Eastern Harbour District Amsterdam

Ai Publishers

Eastern Harbour District Amsterdam

Urbanism and Architecture

Contents

Introduction

The transformation of the Eastern Harbour District in Amsterdam was completed in 2003. More than 8,000 dwellings have definitively taken over from hangars, transhipment installations, rails, containers and goods trains. All of the Netherlands' top architects have built here, as well as a large number of renowned foreigners. An operation like this appeals to the imagination. The number of articles in newspapers and magazines is impressive, as are the numbers of architecture and urban-planning tourists who have visited the district in recent years. Until now, however, there was no single publication in which the entire district was documented in its completed form. Each of the various sections of the district has had a book devoted to it over the years, but only this book gives us a complete overview of the Eastern Harbour District, with historical information and with extensive documentation on every existing project that has by now been built. Besides the built and visible projects, such as dwellings, facilities, infrastructure and public space, this publication also devotes attention to the invisible: the planning process, the basic urban-planning principles, and the cultural and social impact at a local and national level.

A variety of authors, including those involved in bringing about the Eastern Harbour District, as well as leading Dutch critics, shed light on these themes.

The separate areas within the harbour district are presented in separate chapters and are provided with an introduction in which the most significant facts are listed. Photographs, drawings and the usual project information are included for all the important buildings. All projects, as well as their architects and locations, can be found on the map. All this presents a thorough overview of the work that has been done in the east of Amsterdam over the past several years – and its eventual result. Simultaneously, this book gives a clear picture of how housing construction is approached in the Netherlands, what it means to transform an urban industrial area into a residential area, and finally, how Amsterdam managed to realize a residential district of worldwide fame on a site with tricky access and on land difficult to build upon.

Amsterdam on the sea
The historic development of the Eastern Harbour District

Jaap Evert Abrahamse

The history of the Eastern Harbour District began in the second half of the nineteenth century, Amsterdam's 'second Golden Age'. The advent of steamships and railways entailed a significantly different development from that of the older harbour islands built in the sixteenth and seventeenth century. The enormous length of the docks was necessary for the loading and unloading of large sea-going vessels. The clusters of railroad tracks serving the entire area were another nineteenth-century phenomenon. Yet the islands of the Eastern Harbour District were part of a long tradition of harbour islands, which had begun in the sixteenth century with the construction of the island Uilenburg.

Over the years an archipelago of harbour islands came to be built along the bank of the IJ River, with an intricate infrastructure network – a dynamic area, where rapid developments took place. History shows that the port of Amsterdam has always had a major influence on the development of the city, and that the redevelopment of the harbour district into a residential area dates back as far as the sixteenth century.

Economic renaissance under the Republic in the sixteenth and seventeenth century is traditionally attributed to the development of trade and shipping. The Amsterdam seaport, from early on the largest in the Netherlands, played a big part in this. The hundreds of city views made of Amsterdam show the IJ in the foreground, crowded with vessels; behind that we see the packed harbour (the 'forest of masts'), and only then does the silhouette of the city come into view. The interweaving of city and port was well rendered in the description of Amsterdam published by the historian Filips von Zesen in 1664. He referred to city expansion and ship-building in the same breath: to this end he coined the term 'See-bau', or 'sea-building'. In his view the city had not only expanded along the IJ, but, through 'sea-building', over the entire known world, as far as the East Indies.[1]

The position of the city was an important factor in the development of the port. Access from the inland sea, the Zuiderzee, was combined with a favourable location in relation to the hinterland. The IJ, a sea arm protected by a number of land spits such as the Volewijk, was a good anchoring site for ships. The land spits directed the tidal flow from the Zuiderzee and kept the harbour at the right depth. The city had the Volewijk and the land spit to its west reinforced in order to counteract the silting up of the harbour.

The port of Amsterdam played an important role not just in an economic but also in an urban development sense. The port was always in the forefront of the city's development. The expansion of the port area provided an occasion for expanding the city on a number of occasions. The port was always ahead of the city in urban-planning methods as well. It was in the port that a system of urban planning with a mathematical basis was first applied, with rectilinear streets and orthogonal parcels. The dynamics of the harbour district in the sixteenth century led to the first cases of redevelopment: obsolete harbours were absorbed by the city and transformed into residential areas, while new, larger harbour islands were constructed in the IJ.[2] The redevelopment of the Lastage into a residential district in 1586 and that of the old eastern islands in the early seventeenth century are examples of this sort of transformation from harbour district to residential area.

The sea-dike along the IJ

The sea-dike along the south bank of the IJ was the most important element in the urban structure of Amsterdam. On the inner side of the dike lay the city, on the outer side her port. In the city we see housing blocks surrounded by canals. Outside the dike we see an inverted structure of harbour islands, constructed in the IJ. In many places, the harbour canals between these are twice as wide as the canals in the city. The port covered the entire area of the city outside the dike; it was a tidal harbour, directly connected to open water. All areas beyond the sea-dike were at risk of flooding at high tide. This occurred regularly. The Open IJ would not be dammed off until 1872, with the construction of the dam at Schellingwoude.

In the Middle Ages, the IJ dike curved inward towards land at the estuary of the Amstel river, where the Nieuwendijk shopping street now lies; some distance upstream the dike crossed the Middeldam, where the Amstel was dammed off by a lock, then continued its way eastwards across the Warmoesstraat, the Zeedijk and the Sint-Anthoniesdijk (the present-day Sint-Anthoniesbreestraat). The estuary of the Amstel, between the banks of the IJ and the Dam, was thus a sheltered mooring spot for ships. On either side of the city ran the Oudezijds and Nieuwezijds Walen, great ship-mooring docks in the IJ. The IJ was dammed off by a double line of pylons (the 'trees') in order to provide a safe mooring site for ships. These pylons also served a military function, as harbour fortifications. Until the Central Station was built, the city would continue to be dammed off by pylons.[3] The port did not exist on its own, of course: the docks along the bank of the IJ were for the most part used to store wood and tar, and the city numbered hundreds of warehouses.

The Lastage
Initially the centre of the port of Amsterdam lay along the Amstel; the tidal flow of the IJ made itself felt as far as the Dam. The Damrak was the outer harbour, the Rokin the inner harbour. Only a small section of the bank of the IJ lay within the city limits, As the city grew, the harbourfront along the IJ expanded. The Damrak remained an important harbour, but more specialized harbours began to develop on the eastern side of the city. This area beyond the dike was transformed during the sixteenth and seventeenth century into an archipelago of harbour islands, which, spatially and functionally, became increasingly cut off from the city.

This process began with the construction of the Lastage, the present-day Nieuwmarkt quarter, then a harbour district outside the eastern city wall. Here, south of the Oudezijds Waal, the fourteenth and fifteenth centuries witnessed the development of an area in which timber yards, rope yards and other enterprises associated with shipping were established. In the sixteenth century, the Nieuwe Gracht (the present-day Oude Schans) canal was dug and the Montelbaanstoren spire was built. After the Recht- and Kroomboomsloot canals were dug, the Lastage became Amsterdam's most important harbour.

The old eastern islands
In 1586 the city authorities decided to develop the Lastage as a residential area. In 1593, to provide new premises for the flourishing shipping industry, new harbours were built to the east of the Lastage, in the form of the islands Uilenburg, Valkenburg and Rapenburg. On this last island, premises were established for the VOC (Dutch East India Company) and the Admiralty, the Republic's naval force.

Whereas the Lastage, for the most part, had been the result of incidental interventions, the three new islands were the product of a mathematical construction, a highly planned intervention.[4] These islands were given an elongated shape; in the centre of a harbour island, lengthwise, ran one or two streets. Between these streets were small parcels for dwellings. Along the waterfront on either side were dockyards. These were accessible by land as well as from the water. The islands were linked to the sea-dike and connected by bridges.

Western islands
The port was stretching further and further along the bank of the IJ; the length of the harbourfront grew along with the expansion of the port during the seventeenth century. In 1610, less than 20 years after the construction of Uilenburg, Valkenburg and Rapenburg, Amsterdam needed yet more space for the port. The western islands were built – the Prinseneiland, the Bickerseiland and the Realeneiland.[5] Like the old eastern islands, two were oriented in a north-south direction, with another island oriented east-west above them. A T-shaped canal ran between the islands. This canal was about twice as wide as the canals in the city. This expansion put an even greater emphasis on the harbourfront along the IJ, which more than doubled in length during the early part of the seventeenth century.

Hydro-engineering
Like most other seaports, Amsterdam had to contend with the problem of sand silting up the harbour, which made it impossible for large vessels to reach the port. Along with the continuous removal of sand from the harbour with dredgers, of which the city had several in operation, a new solution was devised around 1650: the digging of a canal, precisely along the axis of the sea-dock along Rapenburg. The 'friction' of the water that would flow through this canal was supposed to keep the harbour at the right depth. The Nieuwe Vaart, as the canal is still called, did not help; however, this broad canal remained an important structural element in Amsterdam's harbour district, influencing the construction of the islands Kattenburg, Wittenburg and Oostenburg, which in turn determined the direction of the Oostelijke Handelskade.

Two other elements jointly defined the direction of the islands in the Eastern Harbour District. The first is the line of pylons that ringed Kattenburg, Wittenburg and Oostenburg and defined the trajectory of the Dijksgracht, the Oosterdoksdijk and later the railroad tracks. To the east lay a piece of land called the Funen. East of the Funen, there was another piece of land outside the dike and then the Zieke Water. A summer dike was built alongside this body of water around 1700. As years passed, more land was created by depositing dredgings from the city. This created the kink in the bank of the IJ, which we know as the Oostelijke Handelskade, and the kink between the Java Island and the KNSM Island. On the land that was created, the Stadsrietlanden, the cattle market and the slaughterhouse were established between 1883 and 1887.

Eastern Islands

In the 1750s it was decided to designate the entire bank of the IJ from the city's eastern boundary to the hamlet of Outtewael, which was located near the present-day Tropenmuseum, as harbours. This decision eventually led to the greatest expansion of the city under the Republic, the Fourth Expansion of Amsterdam, between 1658 and 1663. Three islands were constructed, linked to the dock that ran along the Nieuwe Vaart. The Kattenburg island was built on the fortifications that were positioned in the IJ; the kink in the Kattenburgerstraat is the result. This westernmost island was allocated to the Admiralty. Wittenburg, the middle island, was designated for private wharves. Finally, Oostenburg became the domain of the Dutch East India Company, which, like the Admiralty, vacated premises on Rapenburg that had become too small. Because of its huge scale and its combination of highly diversified, specialized commercial activity, this island is considered the greatest commercial complex prior to the Industrial Revolution.

The North Sea Canal

After the Eastern Islands were built, more than four kilometres of the IJ's bank were in use as harbours.[6] After 1663, when the fortifications around the Fourth Expansion were built, Amsterdam stayed within its boundaries for more than two centuries. Only by the second half of the nineteenth century did the city's economic and population growth reach such an extent that new expansions of the city and port became necessary. Prior to this time, plans had already been made to secure the access from the open sea, which had deterioriated as early as 1650. The Great North Holland Canal was completed in 1824, following the earlier rejection of a proposed canal through Waterland. This 80-kilometre channel ran from Amsterdam to Den Helder. It did not serve satisfactorily for very long: new ships were deeper and often ran aground. In 1876,

after a lengthy process of decision-making, financing and construction, the North Sea Canal was opened. This proved a resounding success: from the time it was built the number of ships passing through the locks at IJmuiden steadily increased. The canal was regularly widened and deepened, and the locks were also expanded several times.[7]

A huge pile of sand

In the meantime, the Ooster- and Westerdok had been built directly *in front* of the city in 1832 and 1834. In the open Harbourfront, the space between these docks, the water was still and slowly silting up. But a far more important factor was that the existing harbours had been made largely unusable for larger ships by the construction of the railroad tracks and the building of the Central Station: 'By now a huge pile of sand had been created in front of the city', wrote M.G. de Boer in his history of the port of Amsterdam.[8] This pile of sand and ring of railroad tracks cut large sections of the port off from the open water; many 'outstanding' warehouses were now inaccessible to ships. The construction of the railroad tracks and the North Sea Canal placed the city in a curious position: the city's accessibility, by sea and by land, had been secured, yet ships had hardly any places to moor, because a large part of the port was closed to shipping traffic.

'A history of suffering': the construction of the Handelskade

Clearly the building of new harbours through 'quick and energetic action' had become a necessity. Yet little was happening; here and there a pier would be built, but there was nothing like planned harbour construction. City engineer Van Niftrik felt that the state, which, after all, by deciding to build the Central Station was responsible for making large sections of the port unusable, should build a new trading dock near the Oosterdok. The government, however, was only prepared to deepen the Oosterdok, so that large sea-going vessels would be able to reach Amsterdam via the North Sea Canal. The city, unlike Rotterdam, was not willing to start building harbours on its own. A number of private plans were devised but never implemented during this period. After several years' delay, the construction of a trading dock, or Handelskade, was started in September 1875; four years later, only 400 metres of dock were ready for operation. Moreover, a large part of this already limited space was taken over by ferry services. It was of little use to cargo ships. 'And to make matters worse,' De Boer writes, 'the only large-scale harbour is built on a site in which the levelling of the subsoil makes the creation of docks extremely expensive, where room for expansion eventually will run out, and moreover, as far as possible to the east, making any future bridging of the IJ impossible. This is how the history of the construction of the new harbours became a history of suffering...'.[9] De Boer blames this in part on the absence, during the construction of the port, of a great man like Samuel Sarphati, who devoted himself to the city's expansion on the south side.

Putting the 2000-metre Handelskade to use proved to be slow to get off the ground. The city was unable to find operators for the dock. It was too hazardous for flat-bottomed boats and other small ships, because of the sea-swell in the IJ. Nor were enterprises very keen to build on a surface that had just been laid down. The risk of subsidence seems to have played a role here. Apart from this, it had been decreed from the start that the head of the Handelskade would be used by the city for all manner of services, such as the pilotage service, police, taxation, and post and telegraph service. Only toward the end of the 1880s did building on the Handelskade begin in earnest; the first large warehouses date from this period. Until the construction of the IJkade, the Handelskade was the centre of the Amsterdam seaport. In the twentieth century, the Binnenhaven (Inner Harbour), which separated the Handels-kade from the city, was filled in to permit the widening of the railroad tracks along the Oosterdoksdijk.

Petroleumhaven and Houthaven: harbours toward the west

The first oil well was drilled in 1859; in the years that followed a number of major accidents occurred during the transport and storage of 'rock oil' in ports abroad, including that of Antwerp, in which petroleum ships exploded.[10] Fears of a disaster reigned in Amsterdam as well; the Rijksmuseum, then housed in the Trippenhuis, was one of the parties that pressed for the establishment of a petroleum depot. The reason: large numbers of barrels of petroleum were also stored on the docks along the Kloveniersburgwal, and a catastrophe might result in grave damage to the nation's art treasures.[11] In 1867 stor-age within the city was outlawed; an entrepot was built on the Galgeveld, near the spot where the ferry to Amsterdam-Noord now lands. This entrepot quickly proved too small, as well as a fire hazard; infrastructure and facilities were lacking. This led to the excavation of a new petroleum harbour, far removed from

the city, in the Amsterdammer polder; along with the Houthaven, or timber harbour, that had been excavated earlier, this became a significant centre of activity for the port of Amsterdam on the west side of the city.

Transit Commission

Following the 'accessibility offensive', then, the Petroleum-haven, the Houthaven and the Handelskade were fully or partially ready for operation. Yet the port did not really get going. In a 1889 report, the following causes were cited: the Handelskade failed to provide a safe mooring site for barges, the Houthaven had no rail connection, which meant the timber trade eventually moved to Zaandam, and the Petroleumhaven was not yet completed.[12] The report called for setting up a general plan for harbour construction. The Transit Commission, set up by the Chamber of Commerce, was expanded and came up with a cohesive plan for the harbours as well as for barge-shipping infrastructure. The Commission proposed moving the railroad tracks from the Oosterdoksdijk to the south side of the Nieuwe Vaart, in order to make the Oosterdok and the Nieuwe Vaart once again navigable for sea-going vessels. This never happened: the railroad cluster is still situated where it has always been. In addition, the plan, for the first time, included projects for docks in the IJ, north of the Handelskade. The Transit Commission's plan is the first example of a cohe-sive approach for harbour construction; the plan was not implemented in all its facets, but it had a major impact on the later development of the Eastern Harbour District, not least because the construction of harbours was carried out with an eye toward cohesion among these harbours as well as cohesion with the infrastructure. This marks the origin of the present island layout.

Breakwater

Before the islands were built, a 1400-metre longitudinal levee was built in the IJ, north of the Handelskade. This was meant to protect the flat-bottomed boats moored along the dock from the swelling waves in the IJ. Several years earlier a curious experiment with a floating breakwater had failed. The period between 1884 and 1890, during which a number of free-standing docks were built, was one of trade stagnation. Before islands were laid down in the IJ came the construction of the Spoorweghaven, or railroad harbour, on the Stadsriet-landen – existing land outside the dike. Earth excavated for its basin was used for the harbour island now known as Sporenburg. Between 1896 and 1902, the Entrepothaven was built south of this Spoorweg basin, along with the seven warehouses named after the days of the week, from Zondag (Sunday) through Zaterdag (Saturday).

In the 1890s a cautious revival of trade began; gradually the length of the available docks proved inadequate. It started with the ore ships, which got larger and larger and required a dock with proper facilities. In 1896 came the decision to build the Ertskade, or ore dock, and the IJkade – the present-day Java and KNSM Islands. These were built by expanding the surface of the longitudinal levee in the IJ, using the dredgings from the North Sea Canal, which had had to be deepened to nine metres. That same year, a new lock was open to traffic at IJmuiden; the largest sea-going vessels could now sail unhindered into Amsterdam.

'A shudder of greater activity'

The tide turned in 1899: '… everywhere, here and abroad trade is on the increase. The entire civilized world is feeling a breath of brisker life, a shudder of greater activity', notes the annual report of the Chamber of Commerce.[13] The development of the port's German hinterland and trade with the Dutch East Indies contributed to an important extent in the port's renaissance. Moreover, during this period, millions of emigrants were sailing off in passenger ships to the United States.

Access from the Handelskade to the IJkade was still the subject of controversy: the Commission had proposed a movable bridge. However, this would have needed to be so high that trains would barely have been able to negotiate the incline. The Chamber of Commerce wanted a railroad ferry as a provisional solution; ultimately, however, a connecting dam was chosen, fitted with a passage spanned by a permanent bridge. The dam was on a diagonal in relation to the position of the already constructed hangars on the island and the desired rail connection to the railroad yard on the former Stadsriet-landen. The basin east of the connecting dam was made accessible to sea-going vessels with the excavation of a new shipping channel. In 1898 came the definitive decision, and work started on the dam and the harbour islands. As early as 1900, the first large-scale operator of the IJkade signed on, the Royal Netherlands Steamship Company (Koninklijke Nederlandse Stoomboot Maatschappij. or KNSM), which would begin a huge expansion on its new premises.[14] That year, the railway lines to the islands were also put into operation by the Maatschappij tot Exploitatie der Staatsspoorwegen

('Company for the Operation of State Railways'), one of the many rail companies in competition at the time.

Aside from this, the Transit Commission had plans for a second island north of the IJkade. These could not be realized, because the railroad yard was too small and because the harbour bed here was too unreliable: this was where the primeval channel of the IJ ran.

Along with the KNSM, a large number of other companies opened premises on the IJkade, not just Dutch ones, like the Stoomboot Maatschappij Nederland (Netherlands Steamship Company) and the Zuid-Amerika Lijn (South America Line), but also the Deutsch Australische Dampfschiff Gesellschaft (German-Australian Steamship Company) and the General Steam Navigation Company. The port's growth now progressed apace. After the Borneokade and the Zeeburgerkade were built, south of the IJkade, all available space was being used.[15] Yet possibilities for expansion still had to be explored. The Eastern Harbour District offered no such possibilities: expansion northwards was impossible, given the high cost of a rail connection. Therefore the Havenplan-West (Port Plan-West) was presented in 1912. Not only were there extensive sites available in the west, but increasing rail traffic between Amsterdam and Zaandam had turned the Hem bridge into a serious barrier to shipping. In the 1920s it was still thought that the start of the Zuiderzee works would give a new impulse to the Eastern Harbour District. The eastern dam in the IJ would be moved for these works, which would create new possibilities for expansion. The impoldering of the IJsselmeer would create a new province, for which the Eastern Harbour District would play a part in importing and exporting goods.

The end of the harbours

The Eastern Harbour District was not favourably situated in relation to the North Sea Canal. The construction of the Oranjesluizen locks had relegated the direct connection between the IJ and the Zuiderzee to history. After a short but intense revival, things went downhill for the Eastern Harbour District after the Second World War. As industry increased in scale, mixed-cargo transport was replaced by bulk transport and container shipping, which required longer dock lengths than were available in the Eastern Harbour District. The advent of air travel significantly reduced passenger numbers on the great ocean lines. In the western harbours, potential for growth was unlimited, at least as far as the available hectares of land were concerned. The city saw its opportunity. The Eastern

Harbour District was sold to the city authorities; the municipal goverment's coalition programme for 1978-1982 designated the islands as residential zones. Amsterdam now faced a new redevelopment challenge. The islands had several qualities that made them a potentially very attractive residential area. The huge lengths of the docks means the water is all around; living on the water has really taken off everywhere in the Netherlands, and not least because of the redevelopment of the islands. There was also the position of the islands. They were once part of a large-scale infrastructure of water-ways and and massive clusters of railroad tracks for freight trains; after the harbours faded out, they ended up in the lee of the city, in a relatively isolated position. Yet they are located on the edge of the city centre. The configuration of the islands, docks and water has come through the redevelopment virtually unchanged.

From the time the harbours were dismantled, the architecture of the hangars, offices and warehouses, mostly dating from the epic era of steamships, appealed to squatters and artists. After these were driven off to the real outskirts of the city, the architecture of the harbours, as an atmospheric element in an environment with abundant water, turned out to be a trump card in the housing market of the Randstad, the urban conglomeration of the western Netherlands. The low hangars have all disappeared, but a number of other buildings, like the warehouses on the Handelskade and the KNSM's canteen and Loods (Hangar) 6, have remained in their prominent positions. New construction, like the existing buildings, was oriented along the length of the islands. Continuity is also evident in the architectural design of the new buildings. The colossal scale, the massive, uncompromising architecture, the emphasis on the silhouette and the use of dark brick is echoed in many places. The diversity and free layout possibilities of the dwelling floor plans in the current housing typologies mirror the freedom the first informal residents of the islands had, when they adapted the harbour buildings for their own use as living and work quarters. With the redevelopment of the Eastern Harbour District, sea-going vessels have been replaced by a great stream of architecture tourists, allowing the Eastern Harbour District to make a fresh contribution to Amsterdam's international appeal.

1 Filips von Zesen, *Beschreibung der Stadt Amsterdam*, Amsterdam 1664, p. 165: 'Ja nicht allein das erweitern der Stadt und anbauen der heuser brachte den Amsterdammern einen solchen glanz und herligkeit an: sondern es hatte sich auch mitler weile ihr See-bau / als eine ursache des haus-baues / mitten in der schweersten kriegen / dermaßen erweitert / daß er sich nunmehr selbsten bis in das weit entlegene Ost-Indien erstrekte.'

2 M. de Hoog, 'Amsterdamse haveneilanden' in: *Plan* (1987), no. 3, pp. 24-38.

3 On the earliest history of the port, see W.H.M. de Fremery, 'De opkomst der Amsterdamsche haven', *Jaarboek Amstelodamum* 22 (1925), pp. 23-110; J.P. Sigmond, *Nederlandse zeehavens tussen 1500 en 1800*, Amsterdam 1989.

4 See E.R.M. Taverne, *In 't land van belofte: in de nieuwe stad. Ideaal en werkelijkheid van de stadsuitleg in de Republiek (1580-1680)*, Maarssen 1978.

5 See L. Jansen, 'Het Prinseneiland', *Werk in uitvoering* 13 (1962-1963), pp. 171-173. A slightly different version appeared in *Ons Amsterdam* 15 (1963), pp. 298-301.

6 J. Gawronski, 'Archeologie op Oostenburg: De Amsterdamse stadsuitleg en het maritieme cultuurlandschap' in: J. Gawronski e.a. (ed.), *[Jaarboek] Amsterdam Monumenten en Archeologie* 1, Amsterdam 2002.

7 G. Lutke Meijer, *De Amsterdamse haven door de eeuwen heen*, Amsterdam 1990.

8 M.G. de Boer, *De haven van Amsterdam en haar verbinding met de zee*, Amsterdam 1926, p. 182.

9 De Boer, 1926, p. 183.

10 H. Spiekman, *De ontwikkeling van de Amsterdamse petroleum-haven*, s.l., 1958.

11 De Boer, 1926, p. 200.

12 *Verslag der Commissie ter Bevordering van het Transito-verkeer te Amsterdam*, Amsterdam, 1891, quoted in De Boer, 1926, p. 258.

13 Quoted in De Boer, 1926, p. 269.

14 E. Werkman and H. van der Harst, *Amsterdam: beeld van een haven 1870-1940*, Bussum 1974, p. 91.

15 H.L. Scholten, *De ontwikkelingsgang der Haven van Amsterdam, weergegeven door elf kaarten en drie graphieken, benevens een korte beschrijving door H.L. Scholten, onderhavenmeester*, s.l. [Amsterdam], 1934-1935.

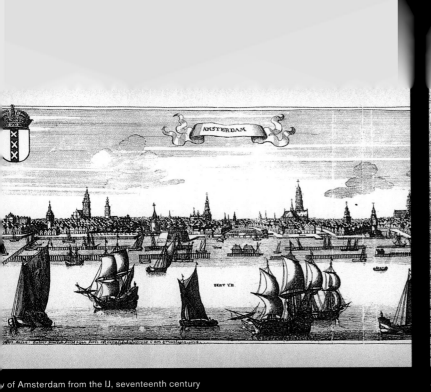

... of Amsterdam from the IJ, seventeenth century

Amsterdam on the IJ, second half of the nineteenth century

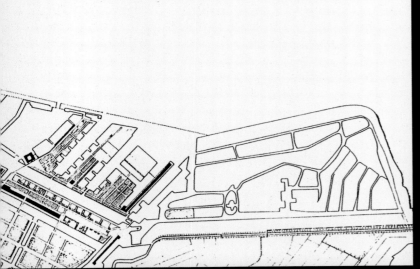

...nstruction of the Eastern Harbour District 1826

1877

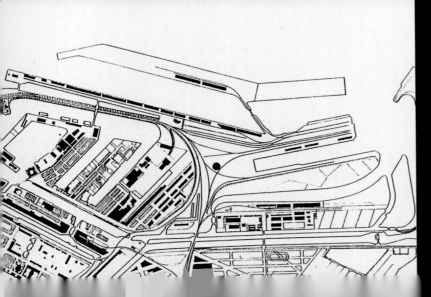
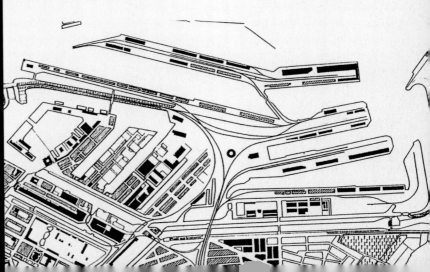

Eastern Harbour District as part of the plan for the southern bank of the IJ, 1989

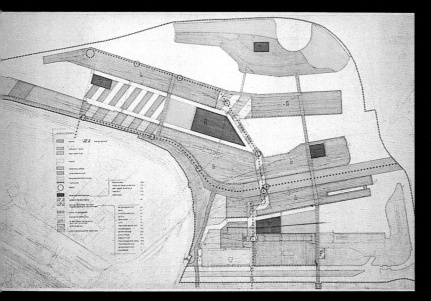

ctural sketch, 1970s

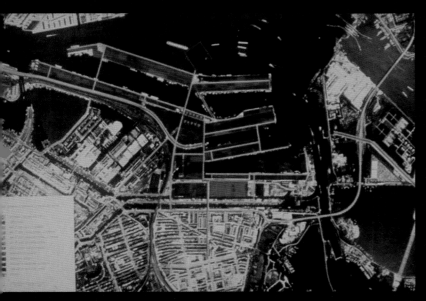

uctural sketch in the Policy Document on Basic Principles, 1990

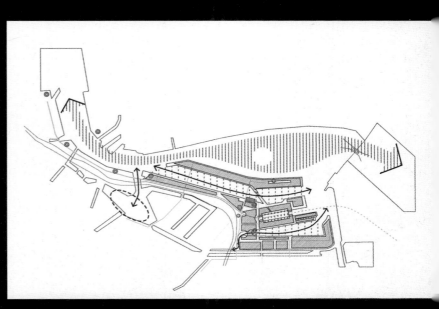

Structural sketch, 1985

Summary of the plan concept in the Policy Document on Basic Principles, 1990

Tail winds

Allard Jolles

The Policy Document on Basic Principles on the Amsterdam Eastern Harbour District, issued by city council decree on 12 June 1985, left no room for doubt: the Eastern Harbour District's function as a harbour area had been in decline since the mid-1970s. From the document: 'as far back as '76/'77, private initiatives made clear to city authorities that developments other than harbour operation were at hand in the Eastern Harbour District.'

Amsterdam's Eastern Harbour District looks so naturally like a residential area that it might be all too easy to forget what went on here between the end of the nineteenth century and about 1980. Harbour activities, of course, but also urban nomads, squatters, practice spaces, alternative art – in short, everything that now comes under the header of cultural breeding ground. The Eastern Harbour District facilitated, experienced and survived it all. And now it seems as if the engineering ingenuity of the nineteenth century had been set down as a foundation for the urban planning and architecture of the turn of the millenium. It seems as if housing was built, infrastructure installed, facilities put in place and employment provided here without so much as batting an eye. This is of course not the case, though the tide happened to be at its flood as far as housing construction was concerned. The period in which the harbour district fell into obsolescence was characterized by intense pressure on the housing market and a revival in urban regeneration. The economy was in a downturn, and industrial areas were there for the taking. If – but there is no such thing as 'if' in urban planning – circumstances had been different, the Eastern Harbour District would not have become a residential area – or only a part of it would have. During the construction, and particularly between 1996 and 2000, the tide had turned; the economy was booming. The average household had more disposable income, and a greater need for owner-occupied single-family dwellings naturally emerged. The housing market grew at an unprecedented rate; even in places where it had once been doubtful that houses would ever stand, the price of a home doubled in a single year. Government also changed. During the first cautious steps in the planning process around 1978, the city government was still a highly regulatory and prescriptive institution, with public housing construction as its first priority. Ten years later, public-private partnership had become common-place. This climate was another factor in favour of market-driven development of a large number of owner-occupied dwellings.

The Eastern Harbour District managed to benefit from every opportunity that presented itself and ride out every societal, political and economic shift, and in doing so developed into one of the most successful new residential districts in the Netherlands. It did not look that way in 1978. Yet the discussions, preparations and financial exercises that were initiated then proved of decisive importance to the success of the Eastern Harbour District project.

Inconvenient

The reasons to build the Eastern Harbour District had been legitimate: the Central Station (construction of which began in 1885) had made the Open Harbourfront unsuitable for large ships, and the seventeenth-century harbour islands had become too small. The new harbour district might have been in the east – the North Sea Canal had been opened in 1876, creating a direct, rapid connection to the North Sea on the west side of the city – but the alternation from deep to shallow water made it suitable for the construction of dockyards. In addition, at the time the Zuiderzee inland sea east of Amsterdam still existed; the Afsluitdijk dam would not be completed until 1932. Yet it was not surprising that the district went into decline starting in the 1960s. Bulk transport (convenient for cocoa, an important sector for the port of Amsterdam) required much wider docks than were available in the district. Boats kept getting bigger (container transport) and needed more depth. Most of the harbour-related commercial activity moved to the Amsterdam Western Harbour District or to Rotterdam. Meanwhile, airlines replaced ships in international passenger travel. The Royal Netherlands Steamship Company (Koninklijke Nederlandse Stoomboot Maatschappij, or KNSM) became obsolete. As a result, a number of buildings on the islands were torn down. Until squatters intervened. The Eastern Harbour District became noted for attracting creative types. Aside from squatted buildings, people lived in huts, tents, trailers and caravans. Big campfires could be seen from a distance. Amsterdam was popular in this period. Young people especially flocked to the city, and this was in part due to the greatly expanded university financing scheme. At the time, a city like Maastricht, the capital of the province of Limburg, in the south of the Netherlands, had no university, and the direct train connection to Amsterdam, plus the guarantee that students who lived more than 200 kilometres away from the city would be given rooms, led to a huge surge. Life in the city had also changed since the 1950s. In the past, it had been 'birth-school-work-death' in one city. Father worked, mother kept the house, and children left the home only to get married and start their own families. From the mid-1960s, the Dutch populace became more mobile, and the role of various family members changed (working mothers, two-income families). The age of individualization had dawned, and personal ideas and choices, rather than Christian standards and values, were the order of the day. The city was the ideal place for this salutary self-realization. At the time, Amsterdam was ideally suited for this target population: besides higher education there were many attractive amenities, and living in a squat was free. The city in a general sense became a temporary abode, where you need spend only a portion of your life. It was no coincidence that more than half of the members of the city council that took office in 1978 were not originally from Amsterdam. It had not always been that way.

Among the squatters in the Eastern Harbour District lived many Limburgers. Years later, designer Jo Coenen was nominated by the housing association Het Oosten to produce the urban plan for the KNSM Island. He is from Limburg, and there was an unspoken expectation that his southern accent would be of help in dealing with the residents of the area, whom the city authorities sometimes found hard to handle.

Urban planning is political

Between 1959 and 1984 the number of residents in Amsterdam fell by more than 200,000, from 850,000 to 640,000 (in 2003 there are 730,000). The spill-over policy, successful because many Amsterdammers wanted to live outside the city anyway, led to a housing exodus from the city. The dwellings in the city itself were in dire need of renovation. In this period, average housing occupancy fell from 3.5 to 2.1. For that matter, this dilution is by no means over: about half of Amsterdam's households consist of one person.

With a list of 60,000 urgent housing applications as a big stick, the Urban Development division of the Department of Public Works had its hands full with urban renewal in the mid-1970s. The focus here was entirely on housing, and on finding sites to build dwellings. National government policy provided a basis for this search: the Third National Policy Document on Spatial Planning, first issued in 1973 (the final part came out in 1977) attempted to formulate a policy for revitalizing the city.

There were city council elections in 1978, and among the aldermen appointed at the time were Michael van der Vlis (Spatial Planning and Transport, among others), Jan Schaefer (Public Housing and Urban Renewal, among others) and Enneüs Heerma (Economic Affairs and Harbour Policy, among others). It was a city council with a socially conscious face, and the coalition agreement included a lot about public-sector rental housing, building for the community, small-scale approaches and investigating the potential for residential construction in the Eastern Harbour District. This was a remarkable step, naming a specific area in a coalition agreement. It showed the new city council was serious. This makes sense, as Amsterdam was not exactly in great shape at the time.

The new city executive set to work with alacrity: by 15 August 1978 'an official working group under the direction of the Economic Affairs division was charged with investigating when and under what conditions the Eastern Harbour District could be redeveloped as a residential area.' This is the wording of the Policy Document on Basic Principles of 12 June 1985. In the mid-1970s, a conservation development plan had been put together, in a last-ditch attempt to preserve harbour functions. However, this plan was never submitted for council action, and in 1978, after the afore-mentioned city council elections, 'active redevelopment' of the Eastern Harbour District was on the agenda. 'Active redevelopment' – that makes it sound like anything was possible, as though there were still choices to be made, but in fact it was nothing except housing, housing and more housing.

Bombastic language

The Supplemental Housing Steering Committee (Stuurgroep Aanvullende Woningbouw, or STAW), was by far the most important organ involved in urban renewal. Urban planning as we know it today did not exist in the late 1970s. Master plans from that period were equally aimed at facilitating housing construction. In addition, research showed that there were enough employment areas, and upgrading the Eastern Harbour District as an employment area was considered too expensive an operation. The concept of the 'compact city' made its appearance, as a reaction to the bundled deconcentration and spill-over areas that had preceded it. 'Back to the city' was the motto. The Amsterdam Master Plan Part C, about employment in Amsterdam, issued by council decree on 18 June 1981, named four employment areas that could feasibly be converted into residential areas: Venserpolder in Zuidoost (shortly thereafter in fact built up with classic buildings with entrance halls, public-sector housing, designed by Carel Weeber), the IJplein and its surrounding area in Amsterdam Noord (also shortly thereafter built up with public-sector housing, according to an urban plan by OMA and Rem Koolhaas), the area around Sloterdijk (still an employment area) and, as should be no surprise by now, the Eastern Harbour District. The master plan also noted that in the Eastern Harbour District the emphasis had shifted from harbour-related enterprises and activities to industrial ones, in the sphere of expediting and distribution. From the master plan: 'If it [Eastern Harbour District] is to continue to function as both "dry" and "wet" work sites, construction of extensive facilities will eventually be necessary. Without them the area will become a depository for marginal activities, such as storage of old equipment and the like. (…) Therefore the time has come to reconsider the future of the area. There is sufficient land available elsewhere for any companies in the industrial and wholesale sectors that might potentially be located here. On the other hand, there is an urgent need for replacement space for businesses from urban-regeneration areas. In addition, reinforcement of the housing function in the central parts of the city is a priority, partly in order to strengthen the foundation of the city centre. (…) All these factors and opportunities challenge [us] to come up with a future that genuinely offers a new perspective for the Eastern Harbour District.'

Bombastic language, yet clear, and at the same time an example of the official translation of the compact-city thinking. What is good for the centre is good for the city. The more support for amenities, the better. And building public-sector housing on the parts of the city bordering on the centre was the way to achieve that. Spill-over had to be slowed as much as possible.

Three departments, the plaberum system
Something else happened in 1978 that was to play a part in the relatively rapid completion of the Eastern Harbour District: the Department of Public Works was split into the Gemeentelijk Grondbedrijf (City Real Estate Department), the Spatial Planning Department (Dienst Ruimtelijk Ordening, or DRO) and the Public Works Department. Work on the future of Amsterdam was carried out in cooperation with other departments, in project groups, at least as far as housing construction was concerned. Employment, recreation and transport were clearly of lesser importance at the time. The word 'metro' was even forbidden for a while, and it was the era of the far-reaching small-scale approach. Wherever housing construction was possible, feasibility was at least studied, and in most cases dwellings simply went up. Public housing already had a department of its own, and so a separate alderman for urban renewal was also appointed, Jan Schaefer. He and another important, relatively young party colleague, Michael van der Vlis, gained a significant voice in the city's affairs. Fellow party members who thought in large-scale terms, such as Han Lammers and Cees de Cloe, were leaving or had already left. Schaefer and Van der Vlis proved they really

appreciated Amsterdam. In part because of this, the Eastern Harbour District is as 'new' as it is 'typically Amsterdam'. Imitating foreign successes in transforming harbour districts (London's Docklands, for example) was not the point.

The new departments could get to work immediately. In addition to various policy initiatives for the greater glory of the compact city, great effort was expended in making housing reallocation in the Eastern Harbour District possible. The Grondbedrijf showed its worth by laying the groundwork for and executing the acquisition of the area, in cooperation with the Havenbedrijf (Harbour Department) and the Dutch Railways.

In Amsterdam, municipal urban planning is carried out according to the plaberum system, an acronym derived from 'plan- en besluitvormingsproces ruimtelijke maatregelen', or 'planning and decision-making process on spatial planning measures'. This system, officially set out on 18 March 1980, and still applied in broad outline today, was instituted following the devolution of the Department of Public Works into three parts. The plaberum system operates in six steps.

Phases 0 and 1, the initiative and study phases, consist mainly of a feasibility study, in view of existing policy, translated into a commissioning formula for further elaboration of the plan area. Phase 2 is the Policy Document on Basic Principles (Nota van Uitgangspunten, or NvU), in the case of the Eastern Harbour District the afore-mentioned product from 1985. This states that the goal of an NvU is 'to reach decisions on global allocation and the urban-planning structure, obtained on the basis of research.' When the statement is made official, 'a financial framework is also set out, as a framework to test the Programme of Requirements'; this programme is Phase 3. Phase 4 is the resulting urban plan, in which everything is set out in detail. Phase 5 is the actual implementation of the plan – although products such as a plan for the layout of the public space may also be devised during this period. Phase 6 is the management phase, which, if everything goes well, naturally continues for years. The advantages of the plaberum system are obvious: everyone knows precisely where each person fits within the planning process, avoiding constant re-examination of individual basic principles and the formulation of a new NvU every two years – because of new fashions, trends or insights – while getting no closer to actual construction.

ABC
Often, though, it does not work quite like that. The unique character of a restructuring area like the eastern harbours is one of the reasons for its lacking the 'clarity usually' found at this stage of the planning process (Phase 2), according to

the unnamed writers of the 1985 NvU. Consultations with the national and provincial authorities about phase implementation and financing are in fact not yet complete. During this period, the national government is busy preparing the Fourth National Policy Document on Spatial Planning (which is eventually issued in 1988), and the city, province and state are trying to figure out where the money is supposed to come from – the operating deficit is estimated at about 35,000 guilders per housing unit at the time. High acquisition and site-preparation costs are cited as the most important factors. At that moment, the most appropriate fund to supplement these deficits is the urban renewal fund. However, this is in no way set up for a residential area of this size. Projections for the first construction section are for more than 7,000 housing units, before 1995. And there is a Kompas Island to be built, north of the existing KNSM Island.

The STAW was primarily concerned about when and what. They had devised a breakdown into A, B and C sites, in which A stood for 'can be implemented immediately', B for the short term, and C for 'can be implemented in 6 years' time', the longer term. IJburg, for example, was also a C site, like the Eastern Harbour District. This ABC policy devised by the STAW is somewhat different from the national government's ABC policy, which stood for the right business in the right place, primarily stimulating the building of offices near public-transport hubs.

In 1981, implementation of the Abattoir (Slaughterhouse) and Entrepot component of the plan is pushed forward, and politically sanctioned, in the so-called 'acceleration variant'. The need is apparently so pressing that part of the Eastern Harbour District must be developed as quickly as possible. The city opts for 100 percent public-sector housing in the form of buildings of flats with entrance halls, tied to, modeled on, and connected to the Indische Buurt quarter. The biggest stumbling block at that time is the infrastructure – in a north-south direction the connection to the Indische Buurt and in an east-west direction the connection with the planned A10 motorway and the city centre. The structural sketch from 1979 offers two possibilities: either across Sporenburg or replacing the Cruquiusweg. One remarkable feature in this sketch is the idea of moving the estuary of the Amsterdam-Rijnkanaal and filling in the old estuary for housing construction. A very costly endeavour for a relatively limited number of dwellings, a telling example of the fixation on finding housing construction sites within the city at the time. In the end, it is decreed in the NvU 1985 that the area set aside for the connection between the A10 and the city centre will run across the Spoorweg harbour basin; informally this is dubbed the Island Boulevard or IJ Boulevard (it is now the route of the Piet Hein Tunnel and Piet Heinkade). Whether this is to be a surface or underground connection was still in the air at the time. The main access way continues along the so-called IJburglaan (from the Zeeburger-dijk across the Entrepothaven toward the Oostelijke Handels-kade), along the Verlengde Veelaan and next to the Panama-weg, in the railroad tracks zone. The immensely wide strip of asphalt and public space near the J.M. van der Meylaan, connecting to the Cruquiusweg from the south, is a remnant of the plan to make the IJburglaan the main access way. The façade 50 metres from the road axis – that is the guideline we see translated physically here.

1981 saw the publication of WAS-275, a product of the Werkgroep Aanpassing Structuurplan (Master Plan Adjustment Working Group). A fine product, because it examined housing, employment, recreation and transport in an integrated way, not just sites for housing construction. Yet this product was indeed about sites for housing constructions, in particular how they tallied against one another. The question here was not whether a certain area should change into a residential area, but when, how desirable this would be (including from environmental or transport standpoints, for instance) and what the benefits were. The Eastern Harbour District, entirely as expected, scored very well on all fronts. The report projected 8,000 dwellings (which is how many were built in the end – a self-fulfilling prophecy?), all of which could be completed by 2000 under the rapid variant, while under the slow variant 4,750 units were projected before 2000 and 3,250 thereafter. This was not unexpected either, since research showed that, for instance, the present Java Island would not be entirely free of long-term ground lease contracts until 2023.

The Fourth National Policy Document on Spatial Planning (1988), the 'urban hubs policy document', mapped out a spatial development outlook for the Netherlands up to 2015. Urban regeneration concepts based on the Third National Policy Document, focusing on developments within the city, made way for expansions just outside the city. The related term 'Vinex site' was created by an abbreviation of 'Vierde Nota Extra', the name of the supplement to the Fourth National Policy Document issued in 1992. The approach in the Fourth National Policy Document, however, remained oriented to projects and sites. This fit in well with the work being done on the Eastern Harbour District and the phase the project had reached by this time.

Second Policy Document on Basic Principles
In 1989 a final Phase 2 product came out, the wholly revised NvU, issued by council decree in January 1990. What stands out first is that this NvU's full title is 'Policy Document on Basic Principles for the banks of the IJ, plans for the Eastern Harbour

District'. The development of the Eastern Harbour District is officially discussed as inseparable from the rest of the south bank of the IJ. An interesting development, as is the fact that on several maps in this NvU a section of IJburg is already drawn, the city district under construction today east of the A10 ring motorway in the IJmeer lake. The transport structure benefited from this: the map 'Transport 1, connections with the city / europe' (!) places the Zeeburger Island in the middle, with an A10 junction for an east-west connection between IJburg and the Central Station, a junction for slower traffic on the Zeeburger Island itself (this section of the A10 was, after all, not open yet; that would not happen until 1990) and no less than five crossings in the Eastern Harbour District. A logical, persuasive picture, which the illustration 'transport 2' makes explicit: the city sees this east-west connection over the Spoorweg basin primarily as a combined rail/automobile tunnel (completed in 1997). Sensible: the harbour basins remain open, affording the area's planned high-density building construction the surrounding open space they sorely need, and sparing the flats on Borneo and Sporenburg from a view onto a noise-abatement barrier. This naturally has an impact on the kind of housing that can be built there. This means the diagonal route across the Entrepothaven is out.

Some other noteworthy items in the 1989 NvU are its deviations from the 1985 Structural Sketch: companies are leaving the Java Island faster than expected; an agreement has been reached with the Dutch Railways on a land exchange; access to to the city centre and its cultural amenities is cited as of national importance (Mobility Scenario '87), and the express tram between the Central Sation and the Eastern Harbour District is included in the accessibility plan for the Randstad, the urban conglomeration of the western Netherlands. The Kompas Island vanishes from the map, because of noise nuisance and the danger zone around the industrial sites in Amsterdam-Noord. Facilities line the IJhaven, not the Verlengde Veelaan. There are also fewer of them, now that the Kompas Island will not be built.

In the covenant signed with the state on 6 July 1989, Amsterdam is to get 79.6 million guilders if exactly 5,767 housing units are built in the district before 1995, which amounts to 100 housing units per hectare, 50 percent of which in the non-subsidized or lightly subsidized sector. Amsterdam also gets a subsidy of 94 million guilders for the Piet Hein Tunnel (at the time still called the 'IJ-Boulevard Oost en Centrum'). The deficit per housing unit has been reduced to 13,800 guilders, because more dwellings are to be built in a more expensive sector, meaning less public-sector housing.

We have almost come full circle: the signature of former Amsterdam alderman Enneüs Heerma, from the beginning of this story, is also on the covenant. By this time, he is the state secretary for Public Housing, Spatial Planning and the Environment.

In the 1989 NvU, projections are made based on new urban-planning insights, compared to 1985. The contrast between land and water becomes important. Building construction becomes typically Amsterdam, especially along the docks. And the following basic principles are laid down by including them in a land-use plan:
– the island structure is the foundation for a specifically metro-politan housing and employment environment, as a twentieth-century counterpart to the city's ring of inner canals;
– functions are connected as directly as possible to the public space;
– parking space within built accommodations;
– as many dwellings as possible have a busy and a quiet side, with a clear division between private and public;
– building height between 15 and 25 metres;
– in a few places, high-rises up to 60, and sometimes 100 metres;
– water becomes a recreational element: docks become public space, with landing stages and aprons.
    The Amsterdam Spatial Planning and Administrative Information committee takes note of the NvU on 7 December 1989, its chairman, Alderman Van der Vlis, speaking for the committee. The political leadership is satisfied.

The work of officials on the district is noteworthy for taking optimal advantage of constantly changing policy. Phases 1 and 2 of the plaberum were speeded up in part thanks to the STAW and the compact-city concept. Thanks to the Fourth National Policy Document, it became a housing construction site near an urban hub, eligible for subsidy. These were tail winds, to be sure, but they were put to good use. After a little more than 10 years of preparation, with a sizable stack of paper as the end result, the city's spatial development division was able to start on Phase 3 of the plaberum – an important step, for this is finally the urban programme of requirements. But the 1989 NvU determined, in broad outline, that people would be living in the Eastern Harbour District the way we see them living there today.

Abattoir and Veemarkt sites and Entrepot-West

Main entrance of cattle market, 1958

Abattoir and Veemarkt sites and Entrepot-West, early 1980s

Veemarkt around 1910

Abattoir on the Veelaan, 1931

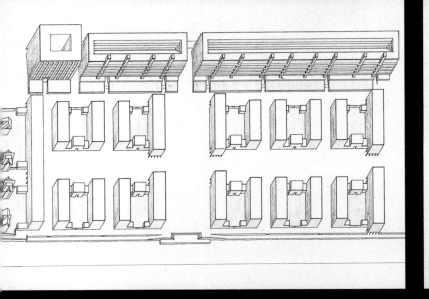

plan Abattoir and Veemarkt sites, 1970s

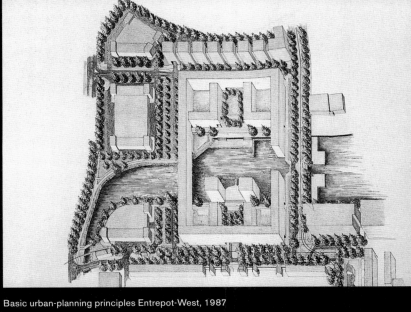

Basic urban-planning principles Entrepot-West, 1987

oir and Veemarkt sites under construction, 1980s

Entrance to the site on the Cruquiusweg

Historic buildings on the Cruquiusweg

Residential buildings on the Cruquiusweg

Entrepothof, looking out onto the Entrepot Bridge

Abbatoir and Veemarkt sites and Entrepot-West
Marlies Buurman

The area where the cattle market (Veemarkt), the slaughterhouse (Abbatoir) and the municipal customs warehouse used to be located, north of the Indische Buurt quarter, is where redevelopment of the district began. The area, abandoned since the 1970s, was an ideal location to build a large number of dwellings within the existing city limits. The plans were devised at a time when the housing shortage was particularly severe, and more and more families with capital were deserting Amsterdam. To counteract this exodus, the city council decided to build housing according to the compact-city model, with a high density of 100 housing units per hectare. The city council also set a goal of making the city attractive to all income groups again, by building larger, more expensive dwellings, not just in the rental, but also in the owner-occupied sector.

This shift is clearly discernible in the approach for the Abattoir and Veemarkt sites and Entrepot-West.

The main objective of the plan devised by the city's department of public housing and the Spatial Planning Department (Dienst Ruimtelijk Ordening, or DRO) for the Abattoir site was the construction of afforbable flats, and the approach was also based on the prevailing urban-regeneration and public-housing practice. Everything was torn down except for the old gate buildings on the Veelaan, and the site was repartitioned. With sun exposure and views in mind, the public housing department proposed strip allotments, while the DRO favoured closed building blocks. The plan that was eventually implemented is a combination of both visions. A total of 550 public-sector rental flats were built, in buildings with entrance halls and no more than five levels, in green zones. The building blocks are perpendicular to the central axis of the J.M. van der Meylaan. Lower-rise blocks are set parallel to this avenue. The dwellings in the western section of the site were designed by Frans van

View of the Entrepothof from the Borneokade

Entrepotbrug, a residential building snaking diagonally across the water

Dillen, those in the eastern section by Lafour & Wijk. They housed the dwellings in pastel-coloured blocks, the orientation of which affords optimum enjoyment of the view onto the water and of sunlight. The layout of the residential area, the separate spaces for cyclists, pedestrians and automobiles, as well as the public parking spaces, are typical of the methodology of the 1980s.

After the Abattoir site, the neighbouring Veemarkt complex was set up as a business park. Several characteristic elements were consciously left intact, such as the former canteen building with its clock tower, the police station and the coffeehouse, all in a decorative chalet style. Sjoerd Soeters converted the former customs office into a colourful day-care centre. Old buildings were left standing along the edges of the neighbourhood as well, supplemented by new construction with historical references. A number of low buildings for small businesses, designed by Hans Bosch, were also built on the site. The brick rear façades of the buildings along the Cruquius-weg evoke the former enclosure of the cattle market grounds.

North of the Abattoir and Veemarkt sites, on the Zeeburgerkade, stands a row of identical entrepot warehouses, named after the days of the week, Maandag (Monday) through Zaterdag (Saturday). These nineteenth-century structures were renovated between 1988 and 1991 and converted into 330 state-subsidized owner-occupied flats. Architect Chris Smit replaced the characteristic steel galleries on the front and rear with triangular bays. On the dock side, the cast-iron awnings were preserved, and balconies were added to the top storey. On the Cruquiusweg side, French balconies and logias were added. The 30-metre-long warehouses were fitted with glass-roofed corridors, in order to let sunlight reach the heart of the buildings. Most of the flats are accessed from these corridors. West of the strip of buildings stands the former tea and herb warehouse Zondag (Sunday), in which Pieter Weeda housed 60 three-room owner-occupied flats. In the centre of the square building is an open courtyard. On the corner of the Cruquiusweg and the Van Eesterenlaan stands Cacaopakhuis Koning

Entrepot warehouses on the Zeeburgerkade

View of the Zeeburgerkade from the Borneokade

Hildo Kropplein, looking out onto the entrepot warehouses on the Zeeburgerkade

Willem I, a cocoa warehouse built in 1961. The massive building was converted by Atelier PRO into the offices and archives repository of the International Institute for Social History. The thick concrete outer walls were pierced in several places in order to provide natural light. On the water side, for example, a great empty space was created for various public functions, including an exhibition space.

The development of the area west of the Entrepothaven, Entrepot-West, marked the turning point from socially engaged building for the community to building for the market. At the same time, the city and the planners recognized the importance of architectural beauty and urban-planning allure. Henceforth residential environments had to be created in order to attract consumers. The outdated residential concepts of the Abbatoir site were abandoned, and the DRO looked for a more urban parcel allotment and construction, better suited to the situation. The experience of the Abbatoir site and the need for a more seductive image led to five architecture firms being commissioned

to elaborate the DRO's concept of a rectangular building block across the water, with a sheltered inner courtyard.

The winning plan was submitted by Atelier PRO. The firm designed a semi-open parcel allotment with both low-rise and high-rise buildings. PRO transformed the building block so that the boundary between the area and the surrounding neighbourhoods was less defined and the external space was more variegated. The area's most eye-catching feature is a residential building of 435 public-sector rental flats distributed over five storeys, snaking diagonally across the water. The building forms a bridge over the water, keeping the Entrepothaven open and allowing small boats to sail under the structure. A second diagonal is formed the towers of owner-occupied apartments situated on either side of the snaking structure. Clever floor plans afford more than two-thirds of the flats in the towers views in three compass directions. A few years later, a 60-metre tower was built next to the Entrepot Bridge, for private-sector owner-occupied flats. At the city's insistence,

Entrance to the site on the Veelaan

Construction site on the Zeeburgerpad

The H.A.J. Baanderskade and the Nieuwevaart

Entrance to the site on the Veelaan, with the H.A.J. Baanderskade on the right

the more than 600 flats built in Entrepot-West included both rental and owner-occupied units and were executed in a variety of housing types. A great deal of energy and money was also invested in the layout of the public space and in creating residential streets sheltered from automobile traffic. More variation in the use of materials was also sought for the paving of streets and the dock walls, and a start was made on the recycling of existing materials and elements in the area, something that was carried on in the development of the islands that followed. For example, the loading platform along the Cruquiusweg was preserved and given a new role as a strolling promenade, and artist Joep van Lieshout renovated the small industrial building attached to it.

The development of the Abattoir and Veemarkt sites, as well as of Entrepot-West, gave the city needed experience in transforming a former employment area into a new residential district. The method, in which the city sets out an urban-planning proposal, followed by an elaboration of the

plan by an outside architect or urban planner, would also be applied to the following sections of the district.

2003

1 architecture firm **Architektenburo L. Lafour & R. Wijk** project architect **Lucien Lafour, Rikkert Wijk** project **dwellings on former Abattoir site** programme **313 dwellings (public-sector rental)**
client **Onze Woning housing association, Amsterdam** design/completion **1986/1989**

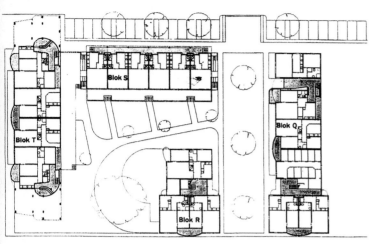

ground floor

9 architecture firm **Atelier PRO architekten**   project architect **Hans van Beek with the participation of Frans Dirks**   project **Entrepot-West and water tower**   programme **44 dwellings (private sector), 221 dwellings (public-sector rental) and 2 parking garages**   client **De Doelen housing association, Amsterdam, on behalf of Het Westen housing corporation, Amsterdam**   design/completion **1988/1991**

4 architecture firm **Hans Bosch**   project architect **Hans Bosch**   project **Veemarkt commercial construction 1st phase and 2nd phase**   programme **commercial construction**

client **Maatschappij van Bedrijfsobjekten MBO**   design/completion **1981/1982 (1st phase), 1989/1990 (2nd phase)**

7 architecture firm **Atelier PRO architekten** project architect **Hans van Beek, Henk van der Leeden** project **IISG (International Institute for Social History)** programme **IISG premises (in former warehouse Koning Willem I)** client **Royal Netherlands Academy of Arts and Sciences, Amsterdam** design/completion **1987/1989**

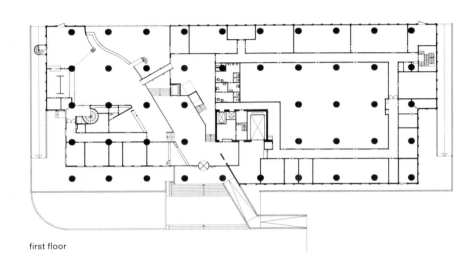

first floor

5 architecture firm **C. Smit**   project architect **Chris Smit**   project **apartments in the converted warehouses Maandag, Dinsdag, Woensdag, Donderdag, Vrijdag and Zaterdag**
programme **330 state-subsidized owner-occupied flats**   client **City of Amsterdam**   design/completion **1988/1991**

10 architecture firm **Soeters Van Eldonk Ponec architecten** project architect **Sjoerd Soeters** project **Oehoeboeroe day-care centre** programme **day-care centre** client **City of Amsterdam** design/completion **1991/1997**

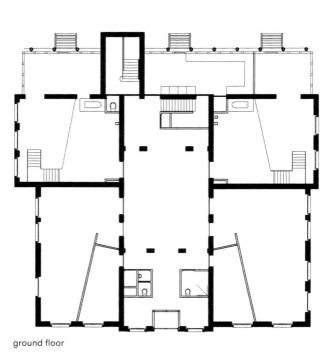

ground floor

Found object
The urban planning of the Eastern Harbour District

Ton Schaap

Everyone has at one time or another drawn lines in the water: it's ephemeral; they vanish instantly.

The Eastern Harbour District, at the end of the 1980s, made an overwhelming impression on me. The big harbour basins, the docks, the railroad tracks, the goods trains and hangars, arranged along lines that seemed randomly drawn in the water; all of it partially disused, awesomely present and obviously ephemeral. It was a marvelous contrast to the enclosed quality and scale of the city centre, the world wonder on the other side of the tracks. What will happen when the qualities of the centre, the 'city', are combined with the larger scale of these harbour piers? High-rises can make the 'wrong side of the tracks' manifest for the other side. It seemed more interesting to try to pursue the urban-planning characteristics of the buildings and to maintain the scale and the spatial effect of the harbour. This kind of thinking led to a Policy Document on Basic Principles in 1989 that contained a phrase about the future of the Eastern Harbour District as the 'twentieth-century counterpart to the ring of inner canals'. This new Policy Document on Basic Principles was intended to replace the old one, from 1985, which had evaded too many choices and was therefore unconvincing.

The Veemarkt (Cattle Market) and Abattoir (Slaughterhouse) sites are under construction at the time as 'supplementary housing sites' and 'inner-city sites for the location of businesses from the urban regeneration areas'. A plan is being prepared for Entrepot-West, the next section of the district, while an intense debate is raging between the city of Amsterdam and the residents of the KNSM Island about the urban planning for the island.

Structure
The questions the 1989 Policy Document on Basic Principles (Nota van Uitgangspunten, or NvU) must answer are 'what is the structure to be?' and 'how is building to take place?'

The Bijlmermeer did not turn into the success it was expected to be, and with this the urban-planning certitudes and some of the credibility of the city's urban-planning department have vanished. Rational considerations such as sun exposure and distances from amenities, greenery and public transport proved insufficient to drum up new enthusiasm for building

in the desired densities in the Eastern Harbour District. Such enthusiasm is needed, because half of the dwellings will have to be built and sold by market players, precisely for the middle-income groups that have deserted the city – where until the end of the 1980s only public-sector housing was built.

Regular systems of roadways and public-transport lines, the basis of functionalist urban planning, are only possible if the harbour basins are filled in. These possibilities have been thoroughly investigated in the preceding years and consistenly result in high costs and uninspiring street maps. The beauty of the semi-deserted harbour district tips the scales at the end of the 1980s: the very form of the harbour district, though not logically suited for a residential district, becomes the most important premise.

More than eight kilometres of docks are available. A large proportion of the required housing programme can be built there, in heights ranging from four to eight levels. Water in front of the dwelling and a sheltered, green inner area behind it seem feasible on all the islands. A unique process, specially adapted to the development of this district, gets underway. For each island, the general basic principles are elaborated by different designers. This creates every opportunity for richly varied construction. The existing structure of harbours and piers is combined with a finely tuned distribution of automobile traffic and the accommodation of the main traffic flow in a tunnel in the Spoorweg basin between Borneo and Sporenburg. A roadway, perpendicular to the piers, will link this and the planned IJ Boulevard.

The 1989 NvU formulates it as follows: 'Around the Verbindingsdam (Connecting Dam), a garland of greenery links a large number of historic fragments. This creates a whole with a new significance, rather comparable to a stellar nebula carrying information from another time.' This puts into words the new programme's radical confrontation with the intact 'objet trouvé'.

In addition to the NvU, a series of montages illustrates the desired development from 1989 to 2000. The basis of this series is an aerial photograph of the harbour district from the mid-1980s. The new infrastructure is superimposed in bright colours onto the photo of the obsolete harbour district. The land uses are shown in transparent areas, so that the foundation remains visible.

Urban-planning inspiration for the islands comes from periods in the twentieth century. The designers base their designs on a concise, clearly delimited public space, to which all functions link up, and a clear delineation between public and private.

In the process of designing a public-transport system incorporating the Amsterdam metro, tram and bus, these means of transport prove incompatible with the dimensions of the harbour piers. The peninsulas are too small to warrant a line of their own. Only the central section of the Eastern Harbour District can be properly accessed by public transport. The tunnel in front of the IJ Boulevard will be called the Piet Hein Tunnel. The minister of Transport, Public Works and Water Management unveils the name at the ceremony marking the striking of the first pylon. This puts an end to the years the tunnel had no name, which had been a deliberate tactic to deny the media and all the people raising objections very much to latch onto. The public debate at that moment is primarily centred on the banks of the IJ, and the Eastern Harbour District can be developed out of the light of publicity.

Shops, schools and a park

In the Netherlands, a developer and an investor usually build shopping facilities together. They demand a monopoly in the area (no shops in the same line of business may be located within a specified proximity) and are granted this for a specified period. This makes a standard, suburban shopping centre inevitable. It is built on the most accessible and most visible location, on the IJhaven, between the Panamaweg and the Verbindingsdam.

Five to six primary schools are needed in the district. Any overflow can be directed to the adjacent Indische Buurt quarter. An equal distribution for these schools will result in maximum walking distances of 500 metres. Later, however, it turns out all the school administrations want to build their schools in or near the Rietlanden, the last area to be built. Appealing to the independence of the educational system, every candidate school administration opposes a school on the Java Island, and no school is built there. The construction of the schools is severely delayed by this, resulting in greater walking distances, and taking children to school by car has since become the norm.

A community park, with a children's petting zoo and a rough playground, is not built 'due to the space it would take up in terms of valuable land and the desired urban density' and because 'this function is to be taken over in part by the harbour basins'. Small-scale green space is placed close to the dwellings on the islands.

Residents of dwellings and houseboats in the area, and squatters in empty office buildings and hangars, support the new approach. They see its qualities, whereas the market players hesitate. The city council 'takes note' of the Policy Document on Basic Principles on 10 January 1990. All the political kinks have been ironed out. The concurrent 'Implementation Policy Document' sets out the financial aspects, including how much the alderman for Public Housing should pay the alderman for the Harbour for the land. This is set at 100 guilders per square metre, which amounts to a total of 26 million guilders (11.8 million euro), in cleared-out but not yet cleaned-up condition.

Implementation

There seems no way to make money out of developing the harbour district. Dock restoration, soil decontamination, bridges, sewers, parking garages and a tunnel all make it more expensive than building on a meadow. Amsterdam has two means at its disposal to implement a plan: land-acquisition policy and public-sector housing construction. In general, land is bought and allotted in long-lease parcels. Every 30 or 50 years the lease is adjusted to the current market value. In this way the city gets a partial return on its investment.

The construction of public-sector housing, dwellings that can be rented out below cost thanks to state subsidies, is the second means of getting construction underway. In addition to the city, the housing corporations play an important role in this. After all, they own much of housing and often have a good knowledge of the local market.

To build owner-occupied dwellings, market players are needed, specifically developers and possibly investors for the rental units. Initially the market is not enthusiastic about building in the Eastern Harbour District. For instance, a developer for owner-occupied flats in the warehouses Zondag through Zaterdag, on the Entrepothaven, was found only after great difficulty in the mid-1980s. And the most important developer for the more expensive apartments on the KNSM Island has pulled out. The conclusion for the planners was that it would be essential to come up with something in the phased planning process for the market players to commit to the project as well.

The city organization gets a project group to coordinate things. Its members represent their individual departments with a mandate. The chairman, Jørgen Bos, a lawyer with extensive experience in the urban regeneration of Amsterdam, manages to unify the Eastern Harbour District project group, and this was important to the approach to the district.

From 3A to 3B

In the same period in which the NvU is put together, an intense discussion is going on about a plan for the KNSM Island. Squatters and houseboat residents retain architects Arne van Herk and Sabien de Kleijn, who live on the Levantkade. They design a plan inspired by the plan by the Office for Metropolitan Architecture (OMA) for the IJplein in Amsterdam Noord. Van Herk and De Kleijn's plan proposes an open parcel allotment in various angles to the dock. This is the diametric opposite of the most recent plan devised by the city's Spatial Planning Department (Dienst Ruimtelijke Ordening, or DRO). The department has devised several versions, but the one with enclosed building blocks and buildings in six to eight levels parallel to the docks wins the approval of the market players, the aldermen and the city council. For most of the people involved, the plan for the IJplein, embraced only a few years before as a refreshing example of new urban planning, is the epitome of what not to do anymore. The designers want brickwork instead of stucco and solid buildings instead of abstract volumes.

Two Amsterdam housing associations, Het Oosten and Het Westen, are the dominant market players. Het Oosten suggests having an architect elaborate the approved plan, in order to make it more appealing to developers and buyers and to arrive at a set of guidelines for a cohesive architectural appearance. The city agrees to the Het Oosten proposal, because it dovetails with the city council decision. Jo Coenen is just at that moment gaining fame for a plan for the Céramique site in Maastricht. This encompasses urban planning with clearly defined public spaces and powerful, rather monumental building masses, primarily in brick.

Coenen makes several designs for the KNSM Island; the last wins the approval of all parties involved. The strong geometry of his design proves its most important characteristic. The buildings that are to be preserved are made part of a clearly drawn system of public spaces and fully or semi-closed building blocks. Despite Coenen's influence on the selection of architects, the intended architectural cohesion is not entirely achieved. Out of a list of 10 architects, compiled by Coenen, Het Westen selects three, and from those a group of future residents may choose one. Theirs is a virtually unanimous choice for Kollhoff. This is the start of a smooth design process that results in one of the most provocative and influential buildings in the Eastern Harbour District. Coenen wants Kollhoff to design a building with an oval inner courtyard, in which the squatted customs office must also be absorbed. 'Das mach ich nie' ('I wil never do that') is Kollhoff's comment.

'Piraeus', as the building is eventually named, deviates the most from Jo Coenen's plan, but entirely matches the spirit of the stipulated requirements – monumental, large, a building instead of a stack of apartments. It is austere, somber, elegant. In material and colour it is at home in the mostly grey atmosphere of the IJ. The programme is encased in a taut membrane of brick, glass and aluminium. This programme is as varied as the city. It becomes *the* city building of the 1990s. Pure in form and detailing, appealing and dangerous at the same time. 'He's beaten us on our own turf', sighs one of Kollhoff's Dutch colleagues at the opening. Kollhoff drew inspiration from typical Amsterdam buildings. He valued the J.M. Coenenstraat, the Telegraaf building on the Nieuwezijds Voorburgwal by J.F. Staal and the mansion offices by Van Gool across the Rijksmuseum. He is impressed by the Amsterdam School and by the lightly constructed brick architecture along the ring of inner canals.

The design splits the College van Mayor and Aldermen as well as the ranks of departmental officials. The proponents of the design win.

'Piraeus' has been imitated many times; it started a new fashion, which can also be seen in the Eastern Harbour District.

It inspires the designers of Borneo and Sporenburg to create their big buildings, the meteorites, and half of the Netherlands design world rediscovers craftsman-like and contemporary use of materials.

The way in which the plan for the KNSM Island came into being is the motivation for a revision of the process that produces such a plan. The most important stage in the Amsterdam planning system is the city council's issuing the 'urban-planning programme of requirements' (the 'stedenbouwkundig programma van eisen' or SpvE). The programme to be implemented, the city street map and the land uses are then stipulated in a so-called 'Phase 3 decision'. But Phase 3 provides too few points of discussion for enticing market players to invest. For that, a complete and attractive picture of the new city is needed.

Phase 3 is split into Phase 3A, still the familiar SPvE, which is the responsibility of the city, while in Phase 3B the full, three-dimensional picture is produced, under the shared responsibility of the market players and the city. In Phase 3A the blueprints and models are made by the DRO, commissioned by interested parties within the city government. In Phase 3B an outside designer wields the pencil, in consultation with the interested parties in the private and city spheres. Selection and supervision of the outside designers becomes an important part of the plan. This process, devised for the Eastern Harbour District after the KNSM Island, resulted in the designs for the Java Island and Borneo and Sporenburg. Organized in this manner, the process yields committed involvement by market players and increases their willingness to invest: after all, they are investing in their own plan.

In Phase 4, the definitive urban plan, each party goes about its own familiar task. The DRO designs the public space and attunes it to the underground infrastructure and the buildings, which are executed by commission of the private parties. This is exactly where the desired cohesion between buildings and public areas comes into play, one of the most important objectives in planning that takes public space seriously.

'Stempels' and canals

According to the covenant with the state, Borneo and Sporenburg are up next. But things turn out differently. At the start of the 1990s, the owner of the 'IJ Island West', as the Java Island was called then, unexpectedly wants to sell the island to the city, 25 years before his long-lease contract expires. The city agrees and is thus able to develop the Java Island sooner. Amsterdam is counting on a cooperative attitude from the state in regard to the number of dwellings to be built – Amsterdam is running behind the contract at that moment. It might be possible to factor in the Java Island. The arguments are many: the sudden availability of the land, the prevention of new industrial use and the opportunity to create a good connection to the city centre via the Java Island, including for the residents of the KNSM Island.

The watchdogs of public-sector affordability step in to prevent Coenen being entrusted with the plan for the Java Island as well. It turns out a great deal of city money has been squandered in the building of subsidized housing in the great blocks on the KNSM Island. It is time for a different approach, with a conceptual basis in the housing floor plan and not in the 'greater form'.

To meet the needs of the new 'housing consumer', the Amsterdam City Housing Department compiles the 'Housing Atlas', in which floor plans are adapted to the diversity now found in the city's households. Besides floor plans, especially suited to living groups, yuppies, students or large families, photographs of the interiors of modern households found in Amsterdam are included.

The Java Island is comparable to the KNSM Island, only 20 metres narrower. The island is the width of one huge building block. Auto and bus traffic will be diverted to the docks, especially the north dock. A new bridge at the western tip of the island, together with the Verbindingsdam, will connect the island to the IJ Boulevard. Buildings will go up about 15 metres from the docks, to spare construction. The buildings are to be on six levels on the south side and eight on the north side. Various studies show that the entire housing programme can be implemented along the docks. All dwellings are to have a direct view onto the IJ or the IJhaven. The middle of the island is made green and free of cars. A bicycle path will run from east to west, as an alternative to the wind-swept docks. These basic principles are the conclusion of Phase 3A, largely in keeping with the 1989 NvU.

How to design attractive architecture on the basis of these simple principles proves less simple. Phase 3B begins. Three architecture firms whose designs are based on the street map and who will not automatically embrace the neo-modernism of the IJplein are invited to share their visions. Rudy Uytenhaak calls the urban-planning principles into question and designs a delicate fabric of low-rise buildings: ground-connected dwellings in small building blocks on narrow streets. The idea comes from designs then being implemented in Nieuw Sloten, a new housing development in the southwest of Amsterdam. It fails to convince the parties, but it will play a part in the discussion about the buildings for Borneo and Sporenburg.

The firm of Geurst & Schulze designs stately buildings along the docks, around a green car-free central area, giving all dwellings direct views onto the water. The Amsterdam aldermen and the most important market player on the Java Island, the Sociaal Fonds Bouwnijverheid, find this plan, although entirely in keeping with the basic principles, too dull. The third architect, Sjoerd Soeters, is brought in to join the other two seasoned housing builders in order to increase the likelihood of unpredictable results. He is invited because of his striking casino in Zandvoort, a quite un-Dutch, cheerful and brilliant mixture of cleverness and seduction, an architectural breath of fresh air in the consensus-seeking Netherlands. And Soeters does indeed come up with a startling solution.

He combines the housing atlas with the urban-planning requirements by introducing 'stempels' – hallmarks or standard building templates. Student houses, houses for wealthy retirees, family flats, lofts, everything is to fit within a façade width of 5.4 metres, which is also precisely wide enough for two parked cars, so that a simple concrete skeleton can accommodate the complete programme, including the necessary parking facilities. Five units of 5.4 metres form a 'stempel', which can house between 20 and 30 dwellings.

Building no higher than a lift limit of five building levels, to avoid higher investment and operational expenses, was quite usual in the early 1990s. One of the problems in Piraeus is that a large number of flats have to share one lift. On the Java Island, all dwellings are made accessible by lift in a well-ordered manner conducive to public safety.

Commissioning several dozen architects results in variation in the architecture of the 'stempels'. Four small canals partition the island into five sections. Bridges connect the sections and create arches on the flat piers and variety along the route from east to west. Soeters' ideas convince the parties involved in the development of the island pretty much from the start.

Individual front door

The owner-occupied apartments on the KNSM Island attract mainly one- and two-person households. Families with children live in the rental flats on the south dock, according to a study, the results of which are available as the design of Borneo and Sporenburg begins. Here a figure of 70 percent owner-occupied apartments is required to reach an average of 50 percent owner-occupied dwellings in the covenant area as a whole. Yet continuing the trend would result, according to the city, in a one-dimensional population composition, a 'yuppie neighbourhood'. Building homes only for one- and two-person households is undesirable. An idea emerges that it might be possible to keep families in the city with ground-connected dwellings, houses with individual front doors on the street. To households with children and two working parents, a direct relationship between the house, parking space and street is probably appealing. Uytenhaak's submission for the Java Island shows that it is possible to achieve density in low-rise buildings on a higher scale than in Nieuw Sloten, where about 50 housing units per hectare have been built. The density is not up for discussion anyway – there is an agreement with the state: 100 housing units per hectare are mandated. A recently published plan by OMA in Fukuoka, Japan, where 50 housing units are housed on a half hectare, looks promising – on paper at least. And there are plenty of historical examples – the city centre of Kyoto, for instance, or, closer, Amsterdam's Jordaan. Only there, the parking problem has not been addressed, or just not resolved. It will have to be on Borneo and Sporenburg.

In consultation with the developer, the New Deal consortium, an initial design round is organized. Six architects attempt to draw 100 housing units on one hectare of the Eastern Harbour District, each with a parking space and an individual door on the street. One of the proposals includes a double surface area, with housing along residential alleyways above the parking level. Other designs feature the classic ground-floor and upper-floor dwellings, each on two levels, or complex interweavings of houses and apartments. It seems anything is possible. A second round is needed to come up with a vision for both islands together with the material available. Phase 3B is going to play an important part for Borneo and Sporenburg as well.

An architect, a landscape architect and an urban planner are selected. The landscape architect, West 8, is the only one to take the demand for ground-connected dwellings seriously. In 'a sea of houses' stand three 'meteorites'. The houses are located on narrow streets in shallow blocks, the large buildings are strategically situated in relation to the surroundings. The Wall House by the Japanese architect Tadao is proposed as the basis for the low-rise structures; the large buildings are inspired by Piraeus. The model by West 8 is intriguing and convincing.

However, for this number of dwellings, the Wall House is neither attractive nor feasible. The ratio of floor space to outer façade is not favourable. The division in slats, 4 metres built up, 4 metres left vacant, allows too little variation in dwelling types; it does not create walls lining the street. Two further studies are needed – one into other dwelling types, feasible under Dutch conditions, to be conducted by Rudy Uytenhaak, and one into the public space, in dimenssions and parking capacity, to be conducted by the DRO. The results lead New Deal to opt for a trial project of 250 dwellings on the head of Sporenburg. If there are buyers for that, further implementation of the plan can be considered.

All the houses are sold, on the basis of blueprints only, in two weekends. Both islands are subsequently developed according to West 8's concept. Their success is unprecedented: upon completion, the houses turn out to be worth twice what they cost the year before, with a wave of profit-taking as a result.

Families with children do choose the low-rise buildings. Another – predictable – consequence is also palpable: the comfort of a private house with a parking space and a foot on the ground results, in the desired density, in a lot of private space and little in the way of a public area. The neighbourhood with the most children has the least greenery, an inevitable and direct consequence of the choices made.

Mikado

The development of one island at a time lends itself well to the twists of policy and the predilections of the market. The harbour district absorbs all the designs as though the islands had been made for them. A sketch from the period around the 1989 Policy Document on Basic Principles reflects the 'mikado principle', a symbol for the acceptance of the form of the harbour district as it was found by coincidence, like the sticks lying randomly on top and next to one another in a game of Mikado pick-up sticks. The sketch is included in the policy document under the heading 'making directions visible' in the 'Concept' chapter. Years later, the transition space between the island follows the mikado principle.

The residents of the new houses demand more green, open space. With an eye to public safety, it is desirable that dwellings be able to look out onto the tram stop in the Rietlanden. With an eye to noise nuisance, these dwellings cannot be located too close to the Piet Heinkade. These three requirements lead to the plan for the Rietlanden. The knot of converging traffic flows is untangled, stylized and absorbed in green fields. The building construction of the adjacent islands is continued up to this traffic hub. The mikado principle proves its worth yet again. The directions remain visible, and so does the whimsical spatial effect that results.

On the islands, the peace of simple geometry reigns, in a stable equilibrium of open space and building mass. In the transition space between the islands, motion predominates; there is a constantly shifting perspective of contrasting elements, building mass and distant vistas. In both instances, the linkage of private and public has been crafted as carefully as possible.

The Eastern Harbour District is now nearly complete. Only the large building on the edge of Sporenburg is still missing. Soon more than 200 Italian poplar trees will envelop the traffic hub in the Rietlanden in a green rustling haze.

The Eastern Harbour District works. Between the Van Eesterenlaan and the Verbindingsdam there are always people on the move now, cyclists, pedestrians, cars, on their way home, to the supermarket, to school or to work. In the distance a train rumbles by, a bus takes the turn toward the Verbindingsdam. The now-familiar buildings stand alongside the old houses on the Oostelijke Handelskade, with their front gardens and privet hedges. The water of the IJ-haven and the Ertshaven, with the sky above and the houseboats in it, everything ordered along lines that were once drawn for a different purpose. Everyone has at one time or another drawn lines in the water: it's ephemeral; they vanish instantly. These, though, will last a bit longer.

KNSM Island

Levantkade, around 1910

M Island, 1980s
KNSM Island, 1980s

NSM Island with the Java Island in the background, 1990

KNSM-laan, 1996

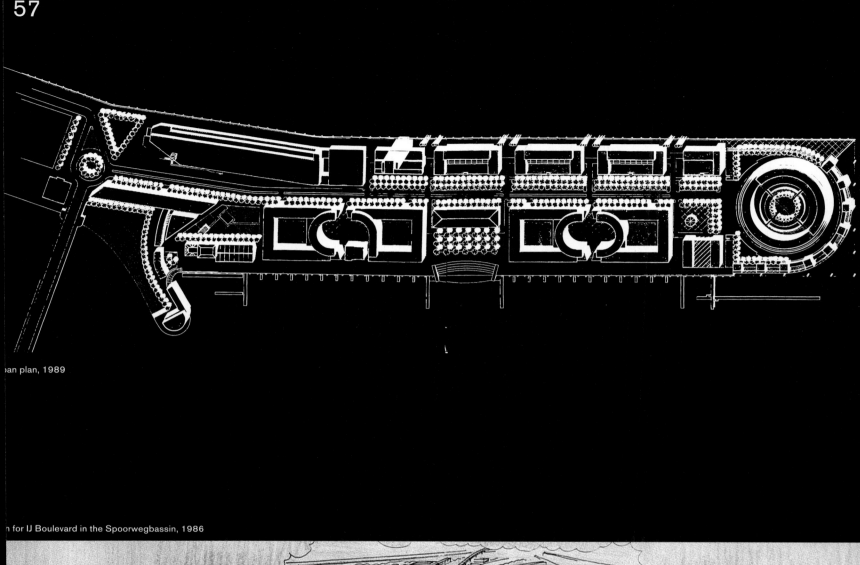

an plan, 1989

n for IJ Boulevard in the Spoorwegbassin, 1986

View of the Surinamekade

KNSM Island
Marlies Buurman

In 1990 the city council adopted a new Policy Document on Basic Principles for the Eastern Harbour District. Its most important stipulations included keeping the harbour basins open and laying a combined automobile and metro tunnel on the bottom of the Spoorweg basin between Borneo and Sporenburg, the Piet Hein Tunnel. The structure of harbour basins and piers were hence-forth taken as the starting point for the development of the district. Following on from this, as many existing elements were to retained, as mementos to the history of the district. In the urban plans for the peninsulas to be developed, classical urban-planning measures were to be applied, such as streets, squares and avenues, and the contrast between land and water would be reinforced by building as much as possible parallel to the docks. These decisions proved to be of great importance to the further development of the district.

The layout of the KNSM Island, the first peninsula of the Eastern Harbour District to be built up, was the most discussed of all the islands. Architects and urban planners started to think about the potential layout of the island at an early stage. The residents of squatted buildings and houseboats moored to the docks participated in the thinking and discussion as well. They supported the building plan that Arne van Herk and Sabine de Kleijn designed for the KNSM Island with financial help from what was then the ministry of Welfare, Public Health and Culture. Their so-called 'Water Dock Plan' is a variant of the IJplein that had just been completed in Amsterdam-Noord and was characterized by an open parcel allotment in which the building strips are positioned in a variety of angles in relation to the dock, so that there is a view onto the south dock and the water from the main roadway in the centre of the island, and not from the flats. The vision of the Spatial Planning Department (Dienst Ruimtelijke Ordening, or DRO) is diametrically opposed to this plan and is predicated on large residential buildings along

the docks and a sharp contrast between these ramparts and the inner areas that result. Many dwellings get a direct view onto the water in this plan. The dwellings behind the dock buildings look out onto an avenue, a plaza or a courtyard. With a little imagination, it can be said that H.P. Berlage's Plan-Zuid served as the inspiration for this first design by the DRO. Alderman M.B. van der Vlis had in fact let the department's officials know that he wanted the Beethovenstraat, with stately blocks and shops.

The city council eventually opted for the vision of the DRO. On the insistence of housing association Het Oosten, which wanted to develop the housing on the island, the Eastern Harbour District project group decided to have the plan elaborated by an architect or urban planner.

In 1989 Jo Coenen was commissioned to design an urban master plan for the island based on the department's structural sketch. Coenen chooses a classic design in which he takes the monumental character of the area as his starting point. A long, central avenue, the KNSM-laan, bisects the 150-metre-

wide island. The avenue is flanked on either side by monumental, high-rise residential buildings and a number of old harbour buildings. Most of these buildings were converted into flats, studios or commercial spaces. The former harbour building of the Royal Netherlands Steamship Company (Koninklijke Nederlandse Stoomboot Maatschappij, or KNSM), located on the north dock, and Loods (Hangar) 6 are examples of this; they now serve, among other things, as the Open Harbour Museum and as a business-gathering building. The buildings on the north dock also include a landmark, a 21-storey apartment tower by Wiel Arets, and four apartment buildings of six levels by Paul and Frank Wintermans. Arets' tall, slender tower, the 'Skydome', houses 100 owner-occupied flats, all with balconies. The façades are clad with dark-grey concrete slabs with a relief, so that it looks as though natural stone had been applied. Deep grooves in the tower suggest that the building is composed of several sections fused together. The verticality is tempered by the horizontal strips of windows.

View of the head of the KNSM Island from the Zuiderijdijk

View of the Levantkade from the J.F. van Hengelstraat

View of the head of the KNSM Island from the Zuiderijdijk

View of the Levantkade from the Ertskade

The balconies of the apartments by the Wintermans brothers are not on the dock side but on the sunny south side, where they take optimal advantage of the sun thanks to the limited depth of the blocks. The south façades are clad in red brick, while on the north side, the unfinished concrete façades provide protection against the elements.

On the island's head stands the circular residential 'Emerald Empire', designed by Jo Coenen himself. The circular shape provides an optimal view onto the water and also creates a sheltered central area. The building houses 224 owner-occupied flats, the greater portion of which are three-room flats. The 18 four-room flats have been placed at the top of the building as maisonnettes. Turning the building inside out, with the balconies, logias and empty spaces on the outer side, has yielded a varie-gated and asymmetrical exterior. The building is encircled by a roadway, the extension of the KNSM-laan, which affords a view onto the IJ between

Two superblocks stand on the south dock of the island, residential buildings 170 metres long, 60 metres wide and eight levels high. To bring life to the whole, shops, commercial spaces and eating and drinking establishments were installed in the ground level of the buildings. The start-up businesses were assisted by a limited subsidy, because the city considered a mixture of housing and business activity important from the beginning. The west block, 'Piraeus' by Hans Kollhoff and Christian Rapp, stands on the dock like a monumental sculpture. The volume of the dark-brick building has been wrapped around the old KNSM administration office. It houses 300 flats, of which a large proportion are standard rental flats and a number are special and more expensive apartments – a differentiation in no way indicated by the façade. The careful detailing of the windows stands out, with their narrow steel frames, as well as the wooden portals that give the building a chic character. A work of art by Arno van der Mark has been incorporated in an entrance gate on the west façade. Pillars bear fragments of a map of Paris

View of the head of the KNSM Island

with a photo of a building or a street in each fragment. In the evening the lamps come on, and the paper city is illuminated.

The adjacent building by Bruno Albert has a round plaza in its centre with a monumental trellis by Narcisse Tordoir in the south entrance gate. The original idea to make the plazas in the two superblocks public spaces with shops and terraces, among other things, proved too romantic. In fact, in the plaza in Albert's residential complex, measures had to be taken to absorb the echoing noise and keep people out of the middle of the plaza.

The layout of the public space on the KNSM Island is remarkable. The design by the DRO attempted to create a connection to the former harbour activities of the area. The street profiles are simple, the materials used in paving them, including Belgian hard stone and the rusty steel-reinforced concrete slabs, are sober and solid. Level variations underscore the separation between new and old buildings and also serve as subtle anti-parking barriers. Next to the Piraeus, for example, is the so-called water

pavement, a sunken plaza sloping down to the water. Mooring places for small boats are located here and at various other places on the south dock. The sunny and informal character of the south dock is underscored by the warm, yellow paving stones, while the recycled rusty steel-reinforced concrete slabs on the cool north dock evoke the former robust shipping character of the area.

The greenery on the island is concentrated on the central KNSM-laan, which, once the young trees have reached full height, will acquire a stately character, comparable to the broad avenues in Amsterdam-Zuid. Anyone entering this island via this avenue finds the KNSM's small green company park situated in front of the Open Harbour Museum. This was designed by Mien Ruijs in the 1930s and restored in 1994 under her direction.

Great care has been devoted to the layout of the public space, just as it has been to the integration of art and architecture. At the end of the KNSM-laan stands the 'Carrousel' by architect Babet Galis. This is a small structure in

which, under a floating roof, Gemeentelijk Energiebedrijf (Municipal Power
Company) installations have been housed, in addition to waiting rooms for
bus drivers. The public space is also characterized by the dark-blue street
furniture designed especially for the Eastern Harbour District by the DRO.
The benches, the balustrades and especially the anti-parking bollards can
be seen as a modern variant on the street furniture in the historic city centre.
There has also been a drive to keep the streets on the KNSM Island clean
and open, and the residential buildings house facilities for the collection of

or 2 architecture firm **Hans van Heeswijk architecten** project architect **Hans van Heeswijk** project **Connecting Dam** programme **bridge** client **City of Amsterdam**
esign/completion **1993/1996**

86 architecture firm **Hans Kollhoff with Christian Rapp** project architect **Hans Kollhoff with Christian Rapp** project **Piraeus** programme **304 apartments, 143 housing units, shops and parking garage** client **De Doelen housing association, Amsterdam** design/completion **1989/1994**

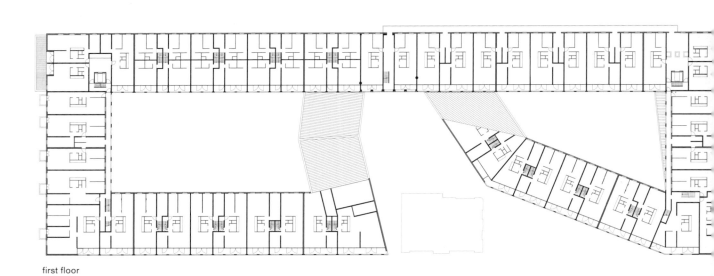

first floor

89 architecture firm **Bruno Albert Architecte & Associés, Buro Heijckmann Ingenieur** project architect **Bruno Albert** project **block on the Barcelonaplein** programme **321 dwellings (public-sector rental), 6 small shops** client **Het Oosten housing corporation, Amsterdam** design/completion **1989/1993**

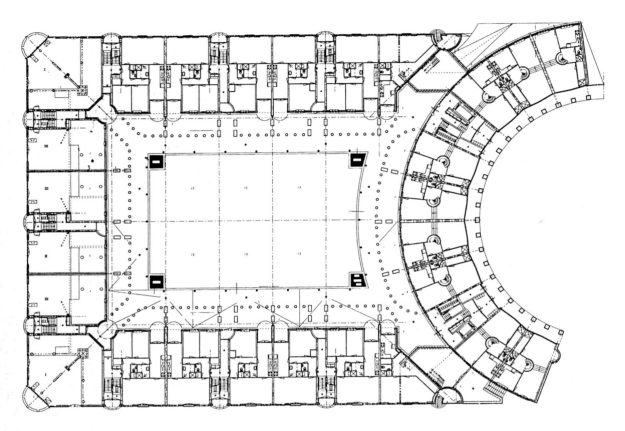

ground floor

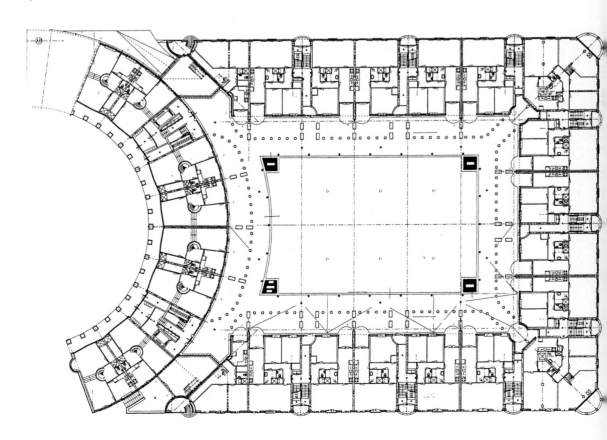

85 architecture firm **Villanova architecten**   project architect **Andries Laame**   project **Levantkade 6**   programme **28 dwellings (conversion of former office buildings)**   client **Onze Woning housing association, Amsterdam**   design/completion **1984/1992**

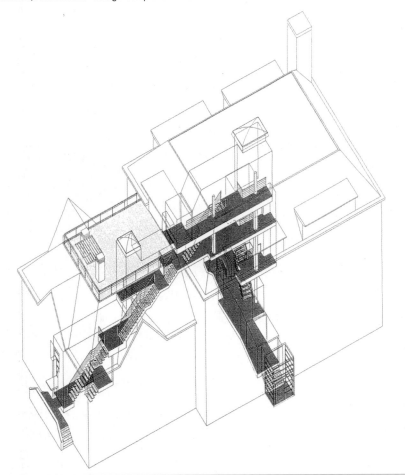

97 architecture firm **Villanova architecten**   project architect **Andries Laame**   project **Loods 6**   programme **commercial space, studios, shops, eating and drinking establishments, museum, art lending and gallery**   client **Kunstwerk Loods 6 foundation, Amsterdam**   design/completion **1985/1997**

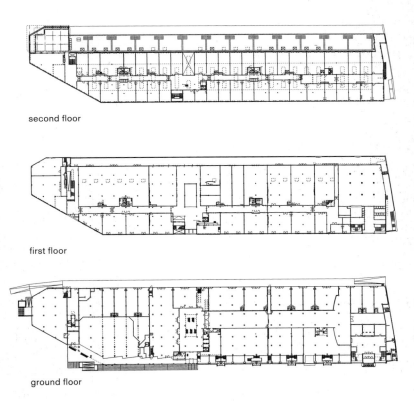

second floor

first floor

ground floor

83 architecture firm **Diener & Diener Architekten**   project **2 apartment buildings: Langhaus, Hofhaus**   programme **172 apartments, 180 parking spaces**   client **City of Amsterdam**

design/completion **1995/2001**

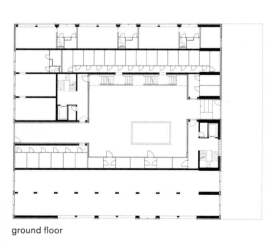

ground floor

ground floor

94 architecture firm **Quist Wintermans Architekten** project architect **Paul Wintermans, Frank Wintermans** project **4 apartment buildings: 1. Archimedes, 2. Socrates, 3. Diogenes, 4. Pericles** programme **183 apartments (private sector)** client **Eurowoningen, Rotterdam** design/completion **1990/1994**

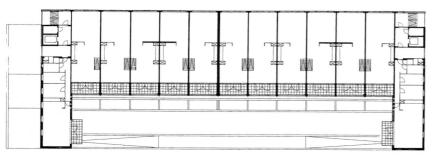

third floor

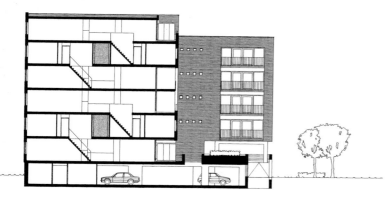

95 architecture firm **Wiel Arets Architect & Associates** project architect **Wiel Arets, Elmar Kleuters, Paul Kuitenbrouwer, René Thijssen** project **Skydome** programme **100 apartments, lobby, parking garage** client **Wilma Bouw, Amsterdam** design/completion **1990/1996**

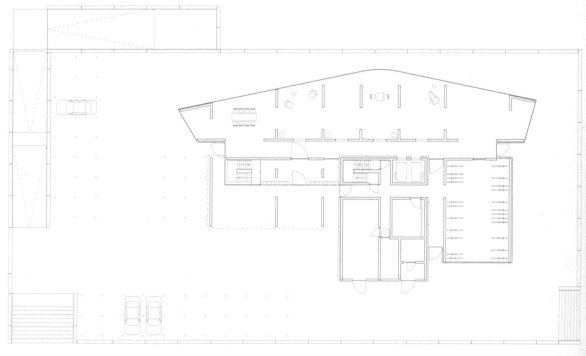

ground floor

92 architecture firm **Jo Coenen & Co** project architect **Jo Coenen, Hans van Niedek** project **Emerald Empire** programme **224 apartments** client **Verwelius, Amsterdam**
design/completion **1991/1996**

Living in the Eastern Harbour District

Jan de Waal

The Amsterdam city council took the definitive decision to turn the Eastern Harbour District into a residential area in 1975; it took until 1987 before pylons were driven into the ground for the first of the new dwellings. It should come as no surprise, therefore, that in 1987 the Eastern Harbour District was no longer just an abandoned harbour area. It was already inhabited by three groups of residents who had very little in common with one another. The first group consisted of the residents of the regular dwellings that had stood in the district for years. Near the Lloyd Hotel stood a row of storeyed dwellings of three or four levels – quite ordinary Amsterdam flats that just happened to be in the middle of nowhere. Captains' apartments stood along the beginning of the connecting dam – spacious flats with large bay windows that had once been allotted to the higher ranks of the shipping lines. In addition the area included some gatehouses and a few company flats, all of them respectably occupied.

Far less respectable, but no less pleasant, was housing in the squatted buildings. From the early 1980s, the commercial buildings that had been left empty by the departure of the harbour enterprises in preceding years had slowly but surely been taken over by squatters. Especially on the KNSM Island, but also on the Java Island, lived hundreds of squatters, for the most part the pragmatic type. They did not engage in ideo- logically motivated physical confrontations with the city, but rather opted to participate in the debate about the future of the district, with a sharp eye to their own interests. The third group consisted of European adventurers, who thought that the Eastern Harbour District signified the final realization of the 1960s' dream of ultimate freedom. During a short but hot summer they occupied the central area of the KNSM Island, from whence the riot police eventually dragged them off, under the approving gaze of the settled squatters, to the enclosure in the Western Harbour District.

The input that these first residents of the district brought to the eventual planning was significant. Until 1985, all city plans for the Eastern Harbour District were predicated on filling in large sections of the harbour basins. This would produce plots of land that were easy and certainly efficient to build on and ensured a good north-south connection for the entire area. In addition, it would create sufficient space for green and recreational amenities, room for which was seen as self-evident in any new housing development. The existing residents called this idea into question with a slogan that has since become legendary: 'blue is green'.

The structured building construction and initial operation of the harbour district unfolded in several phases, in which the housing construction programme changed repeatedly.

Abattoir site

The first phase, which begins with building development on the Abattoir (Slaughterhouse) site, is a continuation of existing ideas about urban regeneration and building for the community. Without much discussion, the basic principle is that at least 85 percent public-sector rental housing is to be built here. On the Abattoir site rises the standard housing type of the 1970s and 1980s: buildings of flats with entrance halls and no more than four levels, to avoid lifts and their associated service costs. In this period, keeping housing expenses down was a priority. The parcel allotment is also dictated by the striving for affordability. Housing construction in strips makes it possible to build rapidly and efficiently and to avoid expensive solutions for corners and angles. The housing programme consists of the standard series of two- to five-room flats, sometimes with a single-occupancy flat on the roof for young people.

Warehouses

The programme for the strip of warehouses is clearly different. The old, deep buildings can only be made habitable after very costly interventions, and hence the city turns them over to private parties. The first owner-occupied flats appear here, in the six warehouses dubbed Maandag (Monday) through Zaterdag (Saturday), in the affordable state-subsidized category. Several different housing types are implemented in the warehouses – single-orientation three- and four-room flats, maisonnettes, and very long apartments with a central area with barely any daylight, but which are very spacious. All the dwellings have high ceilings and are accessible via a lift.

Entrepot-West

The second phase encompasses the Entrepot-West plan. The housing construction programme is slowly altered, not so much because different policy principles are being issued, but because the spatial possibilities of the construction plan are leading the programme. For this brief, the construction of a great plaza above the water of the Entrepothaven, the housing association Het Westen and the public housing department commission five architecture firms. Atelier PRO, from The Hague, comes up with a clever execution of the plaza that includes four slender towers of seven storeys and one tower of twenty storeys – building types that result, however, in high construction costs. It would have been consistent to reject PRO's plan for that reason; instead, the client and the city opted to alter the programme. The small towers house owner-occupied flats in the lightly subsidized and private sector. The 20-storey tower, not built until several years later, houses private-sector owner-occupied flats exclusively.

The late start for the construction of this tower is the result of the complex foundation it required. In the original design, the tower was significantly heavier and would have needed a foundation 60 metres deep. Making it thinner made it lighter. This did mean that fewer flats were built on each level, making the flats more expensive than had been projected. That this tower was built at all can be credited to the rapidly tightening housing market of the mid-1990s.

Entrepot-West accommodates almost the complete housing programme desired in the late 1980s. In addition to regular two- to five-room dwellings, this includes flats for the less physically able (who are assisted by a service facility for general daily necessities, the ADL unit), group homes and housing for young people. The construction of the bridge dwellings directly incorporates facilities for eating and drinking establishments under the structure. It would be several years before a restaurant actually opened in this location.

KNSM Island

Buildings went up on the KNSM Island during the third phase of development of the Eastern Harbour District. At an urban-planning level, a battle is fought here between the adherents of modern building and rational parcel allotment and those who opt for a plan that focuses on the specific qualities of the location. Commissioned by the squatters on the island, Arne van Herk designs his so-called water-dock plan. In it the housing blocks are set perpendicular to the water, so that all flats have a bit of a view, but none of the flats have a good view, of the water. The parcel allotment is very comparable to the plan by Rem Koolhaas that was under construction at that very moment on the ADM site in Amsterdam-Noord. As an alternative, the Spatial Planning Department (Dienst Ruimtelijk Ordening, or DRO), in association with Fons Verheijen, devises a plan that opts for building along the docks. A narrow island between great expanses of water requires a certain degree of shelter, and the enormous quality of the long docks calls for building construction that derives optimal benefit from it. The city authorities eventually opt for the principles of the DRO/Verheijen plan. For the KNSM Island – and, for the first time, out of policy considerations – a housing programme is selected that does not consist entirely of public-sector rental flats. This choice is thus not only the result of the spatial possibilities of the plan, as was the case in the earlier sections of the district. The realization has sunk in that it is vital for the city that higher income groups also find housing there. In the housing programme from which Jo Coenen is to derive his urban plan, therefore, higher-priced rental and owner-occupied dwellings are included from the start, alongside the public-sector housing. The clients commissioning these market dwellings participate in the direction of the urban plan, though

83

they prove rather more conservative than the commissioners of the public-sector rental flats. The APB, which was to have built a few hundred higher-priced rental flats, even pulls out completely, after the bus carrying its board of investors, during its annual tour of the new sites, visits the KNSM Island right at the time that the most vehement squatters are occupying the central area of the island. But other clients are being extremely cautious as well. They limit themselves to standard three- and four-room dwellings, not too small but above all not too large, because there is always a market for these, as the reasoning goes. The towers Wiel Arets designs for Wilma are full of these, and this is also true of the cleverly linked corridor dwellings designed by the Wintermans brothers for Eurowoningen. The flats on the island head, designed by Jo Coenen for Verwelius, are also of the standard type. On this same KNSM Island, building by the housing corporations is considerably more daring. A highly differentiated programme is implemented in the complexes of Het Westen (now De Keij) and Het Oosten. Hans Kollhof and Bruno Albert create huge residential buildings in which very large, very small, very affordable as well as very expensive apartments are housed side by side. Contrary to prevailing expectations, things go very smoothly in terms of occupancy and management in these mixed buildings. This can be credited in large part to the enormous effort invested by both Het Oosten and De Keij in the allocation and management of the buildings. Residents eligible for a flat in these buildings were simultaneously offered a flat elsewhere in the city, so that the Eastern Harbour District could be a well-considered choice. In addition, day-to-day management continues to be bery responsive to this day.

In the midst of all this new construction, five old, squatted residential buildings managed to survive. Levantkade 6 was probably the bastion of the most principled champions of affordable housing. Affordability was the top priority in the conversion of this building from beginning to end. The squatters of Levantkade 8 were already somewhat more advanced in their social careers and turned their residence into a comfortable custom-made accommodation in one of the prettiest spots on the island. Levantkade 10 and the Douanegebouw (Customs Building) on the north side of the KNSM Island, were directly converted into housing and workshops, studios and spaces for non-commercial activities. The most exceptional building is the 'Edelweiss' building, the former canteen building of the Royal Netherlands Steamship Company (Koninklijke Nederlandse Stoomboot Maatschappij, or KNSM). This building on stilts in the centre of the island was squatted by a group of artists who set up their studios there. Normal conversion by housing corporations, given this sort of use, is not an obvious option, and the city decides to sell the building to the squatters. The squatters' conversion plan risks being denied a building permit because it lacks the required second fire exit. By coincidence, the building's users stumble onto six old ship staircases, so that in the end each studio in the building has its own fire escape.

Java Island
The housing programme for the Java Island forms a clear break with the programmes of preceding periods. For this island, for the first time, the question is explicitly raised as to what sort of housing programme should be set out here, without automatically predicating it on the familiar differentiation of urban regeneration with a few market-based dwellings thrown in. In a deviation from the earlier approach to the Eastern Harbour District, it was decided that neither the location nor the urban plan would be the sole determining factor. On the Java Island, a new programme was consciously chosen, which picked up on the prevailing trend. In the early 1990s, the shift toward building for the market was taking place throughout the Randstad, the urban agglomeration of the western Netherlands. In Amsterdam, a series of highly differentiated forms of households and their specific housing needs were described in the so-called 'Woonatlas' ('Housing Atlas'), such as dwellings for hobbyists, for example, with a huge hobby room, or dwellings with work spaces, dwellings for house-sharing groups, or kangaroo dwellings, in which a child or even a parent lives relatively independently in a separate unit within the home. This housing atlas became part of the programme for an urban-planning study for the Java Island by three outside designers –

Rudy Uytenhaak, Geurst & Schulze and Sjoerd Soeters. The programme set out the central urban-planning objective – building along the dock, which would create a sheltered inner area, and attention to good pedestrian and cycling connections. The housing programme was highly differentiated – small as well as large, public-sector as well as high-priced rental dwellings, but also affordable as well as very expensive owner-occupied dwellings, all devised according to the types in the housing atlas. Sjoerd Soeters took this up masterfully. Instead of struggling with it or trying to wriggle out of it, he strengthened the programme by parodying it. Soeters gave each housing programme a face of its own. Along the docks, he placed one building for each housing programme. The building with the flexible family dwellings, for example, is next to the building with the work-at-home flats. The clever thing about this solution is that with it Soeters forestalls the customary objections to the mixing of different housing categories.

On the Java Island, only two buildings met the simple criteria for preservation – authenticity and at least two levels. The SHB building, a former office for the cooperative harbour entreprises, located right next to the Verbindingsdam (Connecting Dam), was converted into a housing and work building. The building on the island's north dock, with the beautiful name 'Einde van de wereld' ('End of the world') was instrumental in directing the planning for the entire island. It stood somewhat closer to the dock than the rest of the buildings, and Soeters therefore included a bend in his parcel allotment, so that the 'Einde' was incorporated into the new construction. When building plans were drawn up, however, it turned out that the soil under the building was heavily contaminated by oil, which could only be removed after tearing down the buiding. The current urban-planning situation, therefore, can only be understood as a form of phantom pain.

The introduction of the lateral canals meant the first construction of canal houses in Amsterdam in 200 years, a housing type that meets the demands of Amsterdammers who really cannot make up their minds. They want a spacious single-family dwelling, preferably with a garden, but they are not keen on sitting in a traffic jam every day between Almere and Amsterdam. The 'and/and' group, whose ideal home is a detached house on the Dam, does happen to be of great economic importance to the city. If the opportunity arises to bond this group to the city, this opportunity must be grabbed with both hands. These little canal houses provided a successful opportunity for this very purpose.

Borneo and Sporenburg

The approach to the next islands signified the next step in the development of the housing programmes. Different housing programmes might have been introduced on the Java Island, but the building form and particularly the relationship between the dwelling and its surroundings were still the same. The dwellings are accessible via stairwells, lifts, galleries or corridors, when it turns out that many people actually like being able to walk into their homes directly from the public street. Any single-family dwelling meets this criterion, but the prescribed density of 100 housing units per hectare cannot be achieved with single-family dwelling. Then, in the early 1990s, the term 'ground-connected dwelling' was coined – homes that are directly accessible from the street but may have other homes above, behind or under them. Adriaan Geuze, of the West 8 firm, translated this programme into the plan area. He designed a sea of houses, each with its own entrance, and in their midst three mega-blocks to increase density and serve as orientation points in the urban landscape. The low-rise buildings are characterized by the ingenious stacking of patios and roof terraces, maximizing the privacy of these outside spaces. About 30 percent of the dwellings are public-sector rental units; the rest falls within the high-priced rental and owner-occupied housing sectors.

Because of goverment deadlines for subsidies and because housing demand is so great, nearly all plans in this area were developed by professional enterprises, housing corporations as well as market players. But in fact the plan calls for each resident to develop his or her own dwelling. This approach was actually selected for 60 dwellings along the inner harbour. The parcels, 4.2 to 6 metres wide and 15 metres deep, were alloted in free-hold to the future residents. They could choose their own architects and develop their own building plans. In a few places, a very small garden has been set on the water's edge, but most of the dwellings have only roof terraces or patios. Inside the dwellings there is considerably more adventure. Some dwellings boast uncommonly free floor plans, in which even the kitchen is executed as a moveable block. An afficionado of old-timer antique cars has managed to create parking space for a row of three cars on his narrow parcel. At the beginning of the street, parking is provided on two levels, by means of a movable loading platform. There is a type that combines a large dwelling with a small one, and there are work-at-home accommodations. Of course there are violations as well: owners of two adjoining parcels who devised a joint plan, with a wide ground-floor/upper-floor dwelling on two levels on the combined parcels. The planning was great, the construction sometimes a tragedy.

The foundations of the dwellings were laid collectively by the city because the dock construction had to be replaced at the same time. On the Scheepstimmermanstraat stand the Amsterdam townhouses of the 21st century, maximized building volumes on very small parcels.

The central area or the Rietlanden

From an urban-planning and programmatic standpoint, the central area is considered a continuation of the surrounding plan areas. Along the Oostelijke Handelskade, the so-called school dwellings are being built. Not everyone was convinced, in the mid-1990s, that it would be possible, given such a density, to develop a housing programme that would appeal to families with children. Educational authorities, in any event, did not believe that there would be enough children to warrant building full-scale schools. However, the number of children in the area has proved overwhelming, and make-shift classroom buildings are being erected all over the place to accommodate them. A more durable solution must be found in the flexible use of space within buildings that, depending on the life rhythm of the neighbourhood, can alternate as housing, schools or commercial premises. The first of these, De Schijf, will be built shortly along the Oostelijke Handelskade.

In conclusion

Transforming the Eastern Harbour District into a residential area has taken a very long time, and in hindsight this has been a stroke of pure luck. Had planning and implementation been carried out according to the plans of 1978, the district would have been completed in the late 1980s just like so many residential areas from that period, characterized by particularly one-dimensional housing construction and population composition. The ADM site in Noord, the former Amstel brewery in Oost, the old Rai site in Zuid, the former fairground in West are a few of the plan areas that were all filled, one-dimensionally, with public-sector rental dwellings in four-level buildings. Early plans for the Eastern Harbour District were also predicated on at least 85 percent public-sector rental units. The planning process also began along this tack. The Abattoir site consists of 100 percent public-sector rental units. Along the way that percentage has fallen to 60 percent on the KNSM Island and no more than 30 percent on Java and Borneo-Sporenburg. This was prompted not just by changing policy but also by two other important factors. The explosive growth in consumer purchasing power during the 1990s made it possible for large groups of residents to buy homes or rent expensive flats. In addition, the residents of the public-sector dwellings, along with the squatters of the existing buildings, laid bare the harbour district and made it habitable. When that had been achieved, the Eastern Harbour District also became attractive for those whose fuller pocketbooks afforded them more choice in the housing market.

It would be sensible for the planning of Amsterdam's great new building sites to take this logic into account.

Java Island

Javakade, 1928

Java Island, 1980s

Eastern Islands with the Oostelijke Handelskade and the Java Island in the background, 1980s

Basic urban-planning principles, 1990

Urban-planning vision of Sjoerd Soeters

java eiland

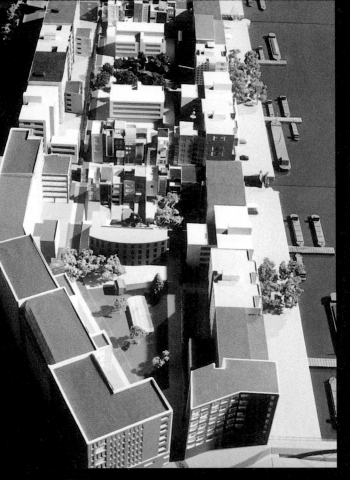

el of urban plan, 1992

View of the Javakade from the Oostelijke Handelskade

Java Island
Marlies Buurman

In the planning for the Java Island the methodology first used in Entrepot-West was continued. The Spatial Planning Department (Dienst Ruimtelijke Ordening, or DRO) conducted the preliminary research, set out the urban-planning preconditions and devised an illustrative implementation. Based on this, three architecture firms – Geurst & Schulze, Sjoerd Soeters, and Rudy Uytenhaak – were then commissioned to devise a plan. The urban-planning preconditions for the narrow Java Island (20 metres narrower than the KNSM Island) included a stipulation that the buildings, as on the KNSM Island, should be concentrated parallel to the docks to take maximum advantage of the view over the IJ and the IJhaven. The creation of a sheltered central area with a bicycle path from east to west was also stipulated, and automobile traffic would be directed via the north dock. The three architecture

firms elaborated the plan in different ways. Although the definitive commission was given to Sjoerd Soeters, contributions by Uytenhaak and the DRO can be recognized in the plan. The idea of building so-called 'Janus-head dwellings' in the central area, for example, is Uytenhaak's, and the layout of the transitional area between the KNSM and the Java Island, with through-views onto the city, is the DRO's.

The master plan by Sjoerd Soeters (1992) differs significantly from the monumental urban-planning approach on the KNSM Island. In contrast to the broad, free-standing residential buildings, here a sequence of different residential buildings has been built, which manifest themselves, with their varied, vertical fronts, as true Amsterdam canal façades along the water. The buildings reach a maximum height of six levels on the sunny south dock and eight on the north dock. A communal plinth provides a binding element. There are public gardens in the sheltered central area and also two free-standing lower residential buildings, the so-called Palazzi. The bicycle path

Head of the Java Island and head of the Oostelijke Handelskade

meanders on the sunny side among the various spaces. The island is segmented crosswise by four lateral canals with canal houses, which partition the long façades into recognizable sections and reinforce the relationship between the two sides of the island.

The buildings on the north and south docks have been apportioned according to the 'stempel', or hallmark, principle. The buildings, designed by different architects, are each 27 metres wide and house 35 to 40 dwellings of one dwelling type, grouped around a central stairwell with a lift. Soeters used six of the lifestyles conceived by the City Housing Department and their corresponding dwelling layouts and housed one lifestyle per residential block. These 'stempels' were repeated in various places on the island. This created a patchwork of different buildings which also expressed the diversity of dwelling types and lifestyles.

The implemented designs include extravagant as well as restrained variants. Soeters' firm, for example, built seven residential buildings, of which the

façade designs of three are among the most striking of the entire district. The most characteristic element of the buildings is the use of bright-coloured panels in the façades, making them function as beacons. The façades on the central area, oriented to the south, are more lively, with their balconies and protrusions, than the closed façades on the north side. One of the buildings on the north dock stands out because of its high portals, which provide a view onto the IJ from the inner garden. On the other hand, the Spanish architecture firm Cruz & Ortiz designed six residential buildings on the docks that stand out precisely because of their restrained quality. The basic design repeatedly shows the same façade concept, with prefabricated façade elements of orange brick with a minimal joint thickness and sandwich panels with wooden plating. The glass openings and logias are cut as continuous horizontal strips in the façade surface. Through their unified façade partitioning and the restrained use of colour and material, they form resting points, as far as the exterior is concerned, among the rest of the architecture.

Brantasgracht

Lamonggracht

Majanggracht

View of the Sumatrakade

The lateral canals are built one and a half metres lower than the docks, which underscores the transition to a more intimate living environment. Lining the shadowy canals with canal houses created attractive places to live here as well. In addition, most of the houses have a back garden and a roof terrace. Various young architects were commissioned to do the designs. They designed canal houses that were repeated and distributed throughout the island. This gave each canal a different appearance. John Bosch and Dana Ponec used the classical concept of a canal house, while Art Zaaijer built a modern variant of the old theme and Jos van Eldonk designed a postmodern house.

The wink that Soeters, with the canal houses, the vertical construction and the variation among them, casts toward Amsterdam's historic ring of inner canals, is made even more obvious by the romantic bridges that span the canals on the south side. The bridges were designed by Rombouts-Droste, who devised a special artistic alphabet to have each bridge represent a different word. The brick-lined car bridges on the north side are by Paul Wintermans.

In contrast to the KNSM Island, on the Java Island no buildings from the harbour period were preserved, except the former administration office of the Cooperative Harbour Enterprises. This building stands in the middle of the park in the transition area between the peninsulas. From here, an uninhabited strip along the south dock creates a sight axis from the KNSM Island, over the IJhaven to the Oostelijke Handelskade and the city centre. At the pivot point of the Java and KNSM islands are two residential buildings by the Swiss firm Diener & Diener, on either side of the Verbindingsdam (Connecting Dam). The complex serves not only as a gateway for the residential area beyond, but also as an intermediary between the differing urban-planning visions on the KNSM and the Java Island. The monotony and the flatness of the façades make the complex a visual resting point in this varicoloured area.

View of the back gardens of the Majanggracht from the Taman Sapituin garden

Perhaps the most spectacular site in the entire district is on the western tip of the Java Island. What should be built on this spot has been the subject of discussion for a long time. For the moment the site remains open and serves as a public-event site with some regularity.

The head of the Java Island is accessed by the Jan Schaefer Bridge, by Venhoeven C.S. This spectacular bridge was built right through the old cold-storage warehouse Willem de Zwijger and connects the island to the Oostelijke Handelskade and the city centre. The passage through the massive warehouse creates an abrupt change of scenery. The spectacular lighting contributes to the unique experience that crossing a bridge can be. Two sections of the bridge are removable, so that during the Sail event every five years, great historic sailing ships can sail into the IJhaven.

Designers for various elements in the public space were brought in at an early stage. This was the case for the afore-mentioned little bridges, but also for the transformer sheds that could not be housed in the residential buildings. Huibert Groenendijk created a design in which he viewed the sheds as 'little chapels from which the blessings of modern technology are dispensed'. They are sober, business-like little buildings, the raised central part of which, with two side naves, is a reference to the construction of a church. Artists were also involved in the design of the portals in or between the 'stempels' and in the marking of the cycle route through the island. The inner gardens of the spaces were designed by the Amsterdam Engineering Bureau in association with the DRO and are laid out and planted as spring, summer, autumn and winter gardens.

The docks are paved with fired paving bricks, except on the south dock. Here the natural stone cobblestones that used to line most of the island were reused. This underscores the character of the south dock, with restricted access to cars, as a strolling promenade

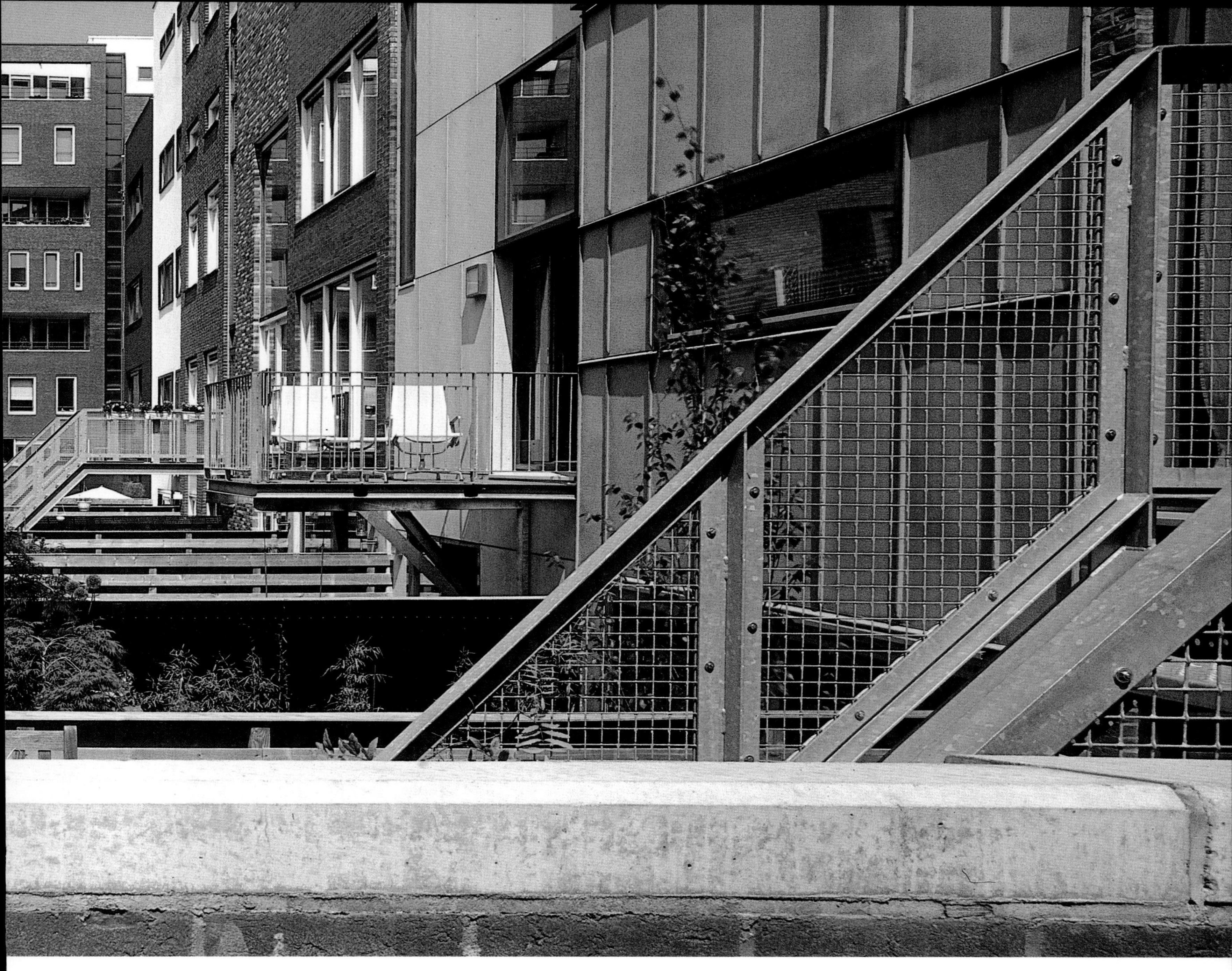

Cycling route along the central area of the island

Cycling route along the central area of the island, via the bridges over the canals

Bicyle bridge over the Seranggracht

Rear side of the Sumatrakade with the Imogirituin public garden

br 3   architecture firm **Quist Wintermans Architekten**   project architect **Paul Wintermans, Dirk Lohmeijer in association with Rombouts-Droste**   project **pedestrian bridges and canals**
programme **9 pedestrian bridges and 4 canals**   client **City Real Estate Department, Amsterdam**   design/completion **1996/2000**

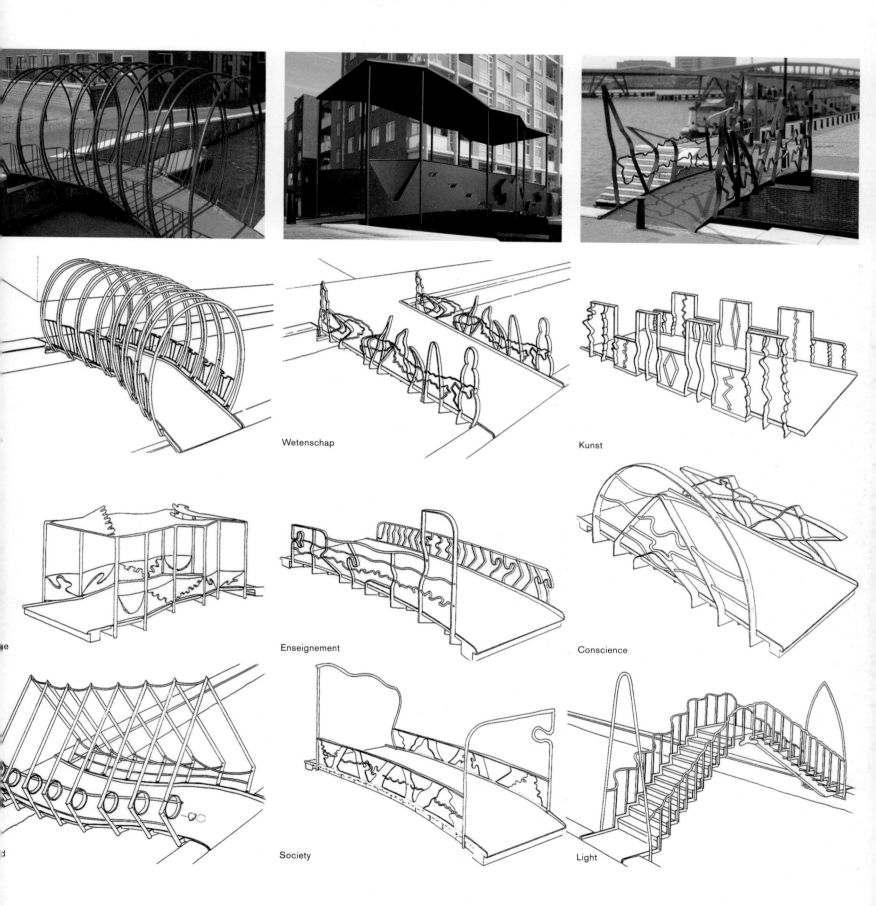

Wetenschap

Kunst

Enseignement

Conscience

Society

Light

br 4   architecture firm **Venhoeven C.S.**   project architect **Ton Venhoeven**   project **Jan Schaeferbrug**   programme **permanent bridge (285 metres) between Java Island and Oostelijke Handelskade for cars, pedestrians and cyclists**   client **City Real Estate Department, Amsterdam**   design/completion **1997/2001**

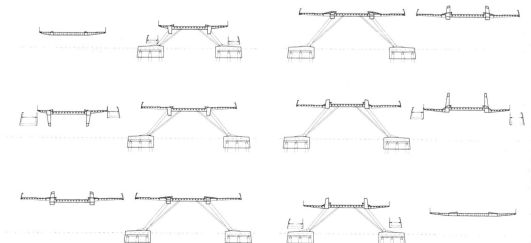

a4 / a11 / b6 / b10 architecture firm **Architectenbureau Marlies Rohmer** project architect **Marlies Rohmer** project **Java Island canal house** programme **4 canal houses**

client **SFB Vastgoed/BPF Bouw, Amsterdam** design/completion **1993/1999**

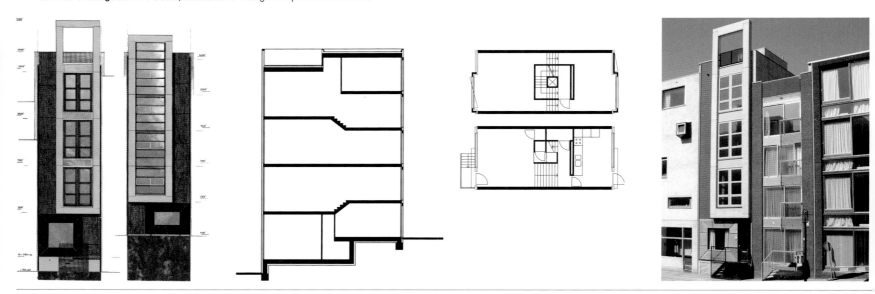

a5 / a16 / b4 / b14 architecture firm **Jos van Eldonk** project architect **Jos van Eldonk** project **Java Island canal house** programme **4 canal houses (private sector)**

client **SFB Vastgoed/BPF Bouw, Amsterdam** design/completion **1993/1999**

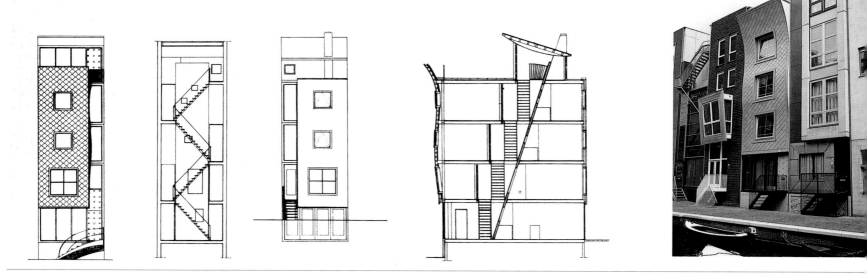

a6 / a15 / b7 / b15 architecture firm **Dana Ponec** project architect **Dana Ponec** project **Java Island canal house** programme **4 canal houses (private sector)**

client **SFB Vastgoed/BPF Bouw, Amsterdam** design/completion **1993/1999**

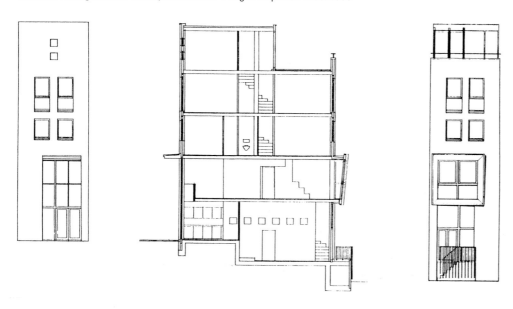

a9 / b8 architecture firm **Bosch Architects** project architect **John Bosch** project **Java Island canal house** programme **2 canal houses (rental)** client **SFB Vastgoed/BPF Bouw, Amsterdam** design/completion **1993/1998**

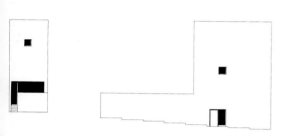

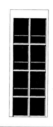

c5 / c10 / d4 / d12 architecture firm **Marx & Steketee architecten** project architect **Annette Marx** project **Java Island canal house** programme **4 canal houses (private sector)** client **Moes Projectontwikkeling, Almere** design/completion **1994/2000**

c8 / c14 / d8 / d13 architecture firm **Marx & Steketee architecten** project architect **Ady Steketee** project **Java Island canal house** programme **4 canal houses (private sector)** client **Moes Projectontwikkeling, Almere** design/completion **1994/2000**

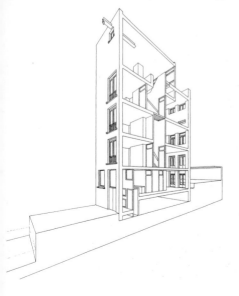

c13/d14 architecture firm **Onix** project architect **Alex van de Beld** project **Java Island canal house,** programme **2 canal houses (private sector)** client **Moes Project-ontwikkeling, Almere** design/completion **1993/2000**

148 architecture firm **AWG Architecten in association with Groep 5** project architects **Bob van Reeth, Christine de Ruijter** project **Java Zuid** programme **18 dwellings (public-sector rental)** client **Woningbouwvereniging ACOB, Amsterdam** design/completion **1993/1996**

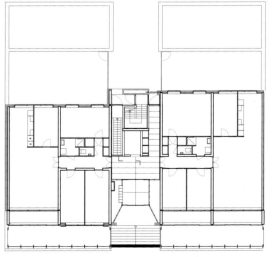 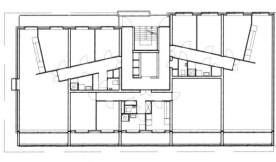

ground floor

first floor

107 / 109 / 113 architectenbureau **AWG Architecten i.s.m. Groep 5** projectarchitect **Bob van Reeth, Christine de Ruijter** project **Java Noord** programma **71 woningen (sociale huur), commerciële ruimte** opdrachtgever **Woningbouwvereniging ACOB, Amsterdam** ontwerp/oplevering **1993/1996**

161 architecture firm **Atelier Zeinstra van der Pol** project architect **Herman Zeinstra** project **Parkblok Java** programme **46 dwellings (private sector) and underground parking garage** client **Moes Projectontwikkeling, Almere** design/completion **1997/2001**

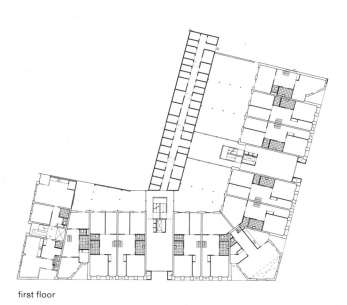

first floor

135 / 136 / 141 / 150 architecture firm **KCAP** project architect **Kees Christiaanse, Han van den Born** project **Java Island** programme **203 dwellings in 9 different buildings, commercial spaces, parking garage** client **SFB Vastgoed/BPF Bouw, Amsterdam** design/completion **1992/1998**

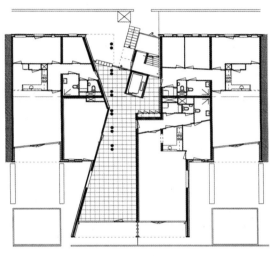

first floor

111 architecture firm **Meyer en Van Schooten Architecten** project architect **Roberto Meyer, Jeroen van Schooten** project **residential building Het einde van de wereld** programme **29 owner-occupied dwellings, 2 commercial spaces, 1 eating and drinking establishment, 1 underground parking garage** client **Olympus Groep (formerly ACOB) housing corporation, Amsterdam, in association with Latei, Amersfoort** design/completion **1997/2000**

104 architecture firm **Soeters Van Eldonk Ponec architecten** project architect **Dana Ponec** project **Java Island dwellings** programme **24 apartments (private sector)** client **SFB Vastgoed/BPF Bouw, Amsterdam** design/completion **1992/1999**

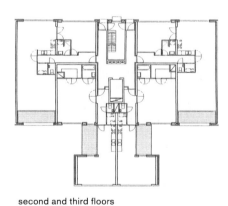

second and third floors

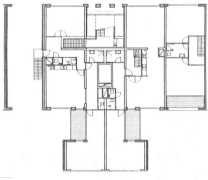

first floor

101 / 103 / 115 / 118 architecture firm **Rudy Uytenhaak architectenbureau** project architect **Rudy Uytenhaak** project **Java Island dwellings**

programme **21 dwellings (101 and 103), 25 dwellings (115), 27 dwellings (118)** client **SFB Vastgoed/BPF Bouw, Amsterdam** design/completion **1993/1998**

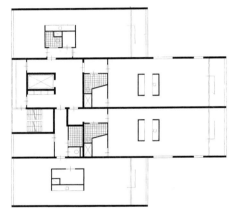

first, second and third floors

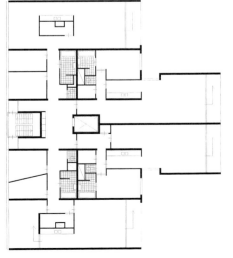

ground floor

99 architecture firm **Jo Crepain Architect** project architect **Jo Crepain, Gert Cuypers** project **Wladiwostok** programme **73 dwellings (private sector), commercial space**
client **Het Oosten housing corporation, Amsterdam** design/completion **1993/1995**

106 architecture firm **Soeters Van Eldonk Ponec architecten**   project architect **Dana Ponec**   project **Java Island dwellings**   programme **23 public-sector rental dwellings, commercial space, heating plant**   client **SFB Vastgoed/BPF Bouw, Amsterdam**   design/completion **1992/1999**

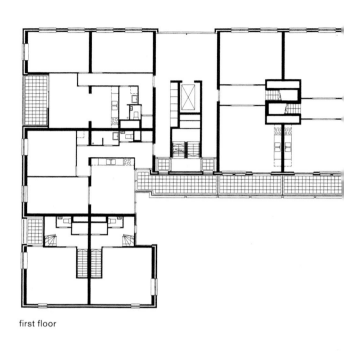

first floor

129/155 architecture firm **Karelse Van der Meer Architecten**   project architect **Joke Vos**   project **Noordkade: Amicitia, Concordia, Hollandia**   programme **81 dwellings, distributed over 4 standard façade 'stempels', 5 commercial spaces (private sector)**   client **Moes Projectontwikkeling, Almere**   design/completion **1993/1998**

153/157 architecture firm **Karelse Van der Meer Architecten** project architect **Joke Vos** project **Zuidkade** programme **51 dwellings, distributed over 3 standard façade 'stempels' (private sector)** client **Moes Projectontwikkeling, Almere** design/completion **1993/1999**

108/110/112/146/147/149 architecture firm **Geurst & Schulze architecten** project architect **Jeroen Geurst (blocks 1, 2, 4, 5), Rens Schulze (blocks 3, 4)** project **Java Island Noordkade (blocks 2, 4, 5), Java Island Zuidkade (blocks 1, 3, 4)** programme **Noordkade: 86 public-sector rental dwellings with parking garage; Zuidkade: 63 public-sector rental dwellings with parking garage** client **ACOB housing corporation, Amsterdam** design/completion **1994/1996**

154 architecture firm **Baneke Van der Hoeven Architekten**   project architect **A.W. Baneke**   project **Java Island dwellings (stempel 44)**   programme **22 owner-occupied dwellings** **(private sector), 2 commercial spaces**   client **Moes Projectontwikkeling, Almere**   design/completion **1993/1998**

first floor

128/158 architecture firm **Baneke Van der Hoeven Architekten** project architect **A.W. Baneke** project **Java Island dwellings (stempel 52)** programme **20 owner-occupied dwellings (private sector)** client **Moes Projectontwikkeling, Almere** design/completion **1993/1998**

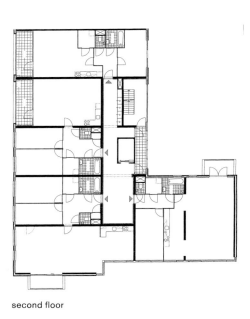

second floor

Architecture as the continuation of urban planning by other means

Hans Ibelings

It is difficult to name a place, in the Netherlands or elsewhere, where so much exceptional architecture has been created in so short a time as in the Eastern Harbour District in Amsterdam. The construction of the entire district coincides in large part with the heyday of Dutch architecture during the 1990s, and it contributed substantially to this flourishing. This area is replete with provocative and significant projects, to which the name of a famous or renowned architect is nearly always linked. The Eastern Harbour District can be seen as a who's who of recent architecture, admittedly not encyclopaedically complete, but with the inclusion of work from Bruno Albert to René van Zuuk, certainly comprehensive.

Dozens of architects with varying visions and backgrounds, from the Netherlands and abroad, have left traces in the district and turned it into a catalogue of urban housing at the end of the twentieth century. Among the work completed here we find various projects that have won worldwide fame thanks to international architecture magazines, such as Kollhoff & Rapp's Piraeus, The Whale by de Architecten Cie., the head of Borneo by Van Gameren and Mastenbroek of de Architectengroep and the Jan Schaefer Bridge by Venhoeven C.S.

So much exceptional architecture all in the same place would be problematic in other circumstances, but that is not the case here. All that beauty and quality creates no difficulties, because there are extraordinarily few ostentatious buildings in the Eastern Harbour District. The significance of the area is in fact due not to the exceptional value of individual buildings, but in the consistency of the whole. Although there are unmistakable differences in the quality of the exterior, the housing floor plans, the detailing and the finishing work, the Eastern Harbour District nonetheless boasts a high architectural average, with surprisingly few notable variances and certainly few in a truly negative sense.

The architecture's high average certainly gives the two most characteristic sections of the Eastern Harbour District, Java and Borneo-Sporenburg, an extraordinary homogeneity. This is where it is most apparent how architecture can be part of a cohesive ensemble that is more than a collection of properties. In these sections especially, the architecture is in many ways a continuation of urban planning by other means. Urban planning dictated the rules; the architecture joined in. It could hardly be otherwise, for almost throughout the Eastern Harbour District the current urban-planning tactic of divide and conquer has been applied, in which many architects are assigned comparatively small projects. This made it virtually impossible for individual architects to tamper with the urban-planning design. In principle, there is nothing to be argued against letting urban planning prevail over architecture; in fact, there is a lot to argue in its favour. The most successful sections of Amsterdam, after all, are the product of a strong urban-planning structure, from the ring of inner canals to Plan-Zuid and the Westelijke Tuinsteden developments.

That the ensemble does not depend excessively on the power of individual buildings applies to all these sections of the city. The best architecture does not devalue the lesser works, and the lesser buildings can cling to and be elevated by the better projects and therefore are barely noticeable. This also applies in broad outline to the Eastern Harbour District, where the weaker siblings do as little harm as the best buildings do good. This is even the case for the hobby-horse of the propagandists of the private commission, the 60 free-hold parcels on the Scheepstimmermanstraat on Borneo. There are a few magnificent houses among them, such as those by Koen van Velsen and by Höhne & Rapp, and a few that are perhaps not as successful, but none of them is out of place here. In the end, the whole is more impressive than the individual parts.

Because the Eastern Harbour District consists of six different neighbourhoods, each following its own urban-planning logic, from which the architecture flows directly, it is tricky to simply make comparisons among what has been built. The architecture of an apartment building on Java is of a different order from that of block of patio dwellings on Sporenburg, and the great buildings on KNSM can hardly be compared to the semi-open blocks on the Abattoir site. Moreover, the neighbourhoods, in their chronological succession, also reflect the different period in which they came into existence, which cannot be easily compared either.

The oldest section of the Eastern Harbour District, the Veemarkt (Cattle Market) and Abattoir (Slaughterhouse) sites, were built under substantially different circumstances from Borneo-Sporenburg, for example, which was completed during the economic boom of the 1990s. The oldest section of the Eastern Harbour District came into being in the waning days of public housing and consists mainly of public-sector housing. At the time, the effects of the economic crisis of the 1980s were still fully perceptible. In contrast, Borneo-Sporenburg, for the most part made up of owner-occupied dwellings, meets the housing demands of an urban middle class that, because of the rising standard of living and soaring house prices, could afford more and more luxury.

The end of the economic prosperity of the 1990s is visible on Sporenburg as well, in the gaping hole on the Ertskade where The Fountainhead is supposed to be built. The initial design for this was done by Steven Holl, who pulled out when he was given prestigious museum commissions all over the world. He handed the project to his Dutch architect partner, Kees Christiaanse. The Fountainhead, which is meant to be the final piece in the urban plan for Borneo-Sporenburg, includes very expensive dwellings, by Amsterdam standards. However, the plan has been shelved for some time. In the optimistic 1990s, it was already an ambitious plan to put apartments up for sale that were comparable in price and size to a villa, but under the current economic conditions, there can be no question of going ahead, and it is uncertain whether this project will be temporarily postponed or cancelled outright.

The last section of the Eastern Harbour District, the Oostelijke Handelskade, currently under construction, will probably also be affected by the economic downturn, with – to use a euphemism for postponement – phasing of office constructions as a likely result, due to the low occupancy rate in Amsterdam, as well as a possible simplified execution of the dwellings, with a more sober variation in housing typology and access points. Typological complexity is one of the most remarkable characteristics of the housing construction of the 1990s, certainly in the Eastern Harbour District, and it is quite likely that the economic malaise that has reigned since the beginning of the new century will result in a more rationalized approach to this diversity.

The Oostelijke Handelskade will consist of an ensemble of large blocks of warehouse dimensions, many with loft-like housing and office spaces, as echoes of the warehouses that used to stand on this site. Here too, a prestigious selection of architects have been retained, like Claus en Kaan, Van Velsen, Christiaanse, DKV, Höhne & Rapp and Köther & Salman, but also newer firms such as Herder Van der Neut and Wingender Hovenier.

The head of the Handelskade, kitty-cornered from Central Station and the Oosterdok Island, forms an exception in its role as closing element, with a programme that consists of a large office building and a passenger terminal, Nielsen, Nielsen & Nielsen's music building and a hotel by Claus en Kaan. Because of these functions, which are related more to the city as a whole than to the neighbourhood, the head has a more urban character than the rest of the Handelskade. The head already stands out in a negative sense because of the architecture of the first completed sections, the terminal and the office tower, both designed by the London office of the American firm Hellmuth Obata + Kassabaum (HOK). In particular, the tower, precisely the tallest building for miles around, is unusually flash, and it remains to be seen whether its immediate neighbours can stand up to so much flashiness.

HOK's tower is one of two architectural low points in the Eastern Harbour District; the other is the uninspired Zeeburg borough office on the Cruquiusweg by H. Klunder. This banal office is located on the edge of the Abattoir and Veemarkt sites, the section of the area where more signs of its former life have remained visible – in the converted warehouses Maandag (Monday) through Zondag (Sunday), in the Koning Willem I warehouse converted by Atelier PRO to house the International Institute of Social History, in the buildings and gates of the cattle market and slaughterhouse and in the little section of railroad, including a platform, along the Cruquiusweg, which now serves as a stone city garden.

The preservation of the original buildings gives this section of the Eastern Harbour District more of an identity than the new construction, which is somewhat on the meagre side here.

The blocks by F. van Dillen on the Abattoir site are the most telling example of this. If any one project can serve as the model for the cold wind of the no-nonsense era under the government of prime minister Ruud Lubbers in the 1980s, it is certainly this one: plain, unadorned architecture of brick and concrete, with plastic window frames as one of the most recognizable index fossils of this epoch.

This architecture is meagre in itself, but on top of that it has reached the critical age at which a building's novelty has worn off, without having acquired a historic patina to compensate. With this in mind, the blocks built by Lafour & Wijk, which went up about the same time, have held up remarkably well. The proper maintenance of the plasterwork in the façades, another index fossil from the 1980s, can be credited in part for the fact that these buildings still seem so fresh.

The partitioning of Van Dillen's and Lafour & Wijk's blocks is also typical for the period in which this neighbourhood came into being. They are semi-closed building blocks with open head ends, comparable to the housing blocks Van der Pek built in the adjacent Indische Buurt quarter seven decades earlier. The closed building block gained new popularity in the 1980s because it was thought this would contribute to public safety. Another reason more closed partitioning forms were such a rage is that an urban quality can be created, with clearly articulated street and square spaces, and this was something to strive for in this period, during which the city and its urban quality were poised for 'rediscovery'.

The same motif was used on a larger scale in Atelier PRO's large Entrepot complex, which was a decisive attempt to give a desolate zone northwest of the old cattle market an urban quality. The complex is an elaboration of a large courtyard-shaped building block, which Atelier PRO draped across the water, making it one of the few buildings in the Eastern Harbour District with a direct relationship with the abundant water all around.

The urban-planning structure of the large closed building block is carried through in the two projects built around the turn of the millennium in the southern section of the Rietlanden, the U-shaped Batavia by Van Dongen and the Geloof, Liefde en Fortuin (Faith, Love and Fortune) complex by Rudy Uytenhaak, which is made up of three closed blocks with a high screen in front that forms the boundary between the block buildings and the random parcel allotment on the opposite side of the park situated above the tunnel entrance.

The difference between the blocks from the 1980s and those from the 1990s can not only be clearly seen in the architectural idiom, but also in the increasing typological complexity. This is to a certain extent typical for these two architects, who rarely avoid complexities, but it is also characteristic of an era in which typological acrobatics almost became taken for granted in Dutch housing construction. The residential building Piraeus by Kollhoff & Rapp and the tower at the end of the Piet Heinkade by Neutelings Riedijk, with 20 housing types in a total of 64 dwellings, are the textbook examples in this realm.

The Entrepot block by Atelier PRO came into being virtually at the same time as the architecture on the KNSM Island, where significant value was also attached to the large urban building block. Out of the whole Eastern Harbour District, this peninsula is the least consistent. There is an inequality in morphology, in dimensions and in the architectural expression. The latter is most visible on the south side of the island, with the almost picturesque postmodern-classical block by Albert on one side of the Levantplein and the monumental rigour of Piraeus on the other side. These two buildings emphasize that it is every man for himself on this island, and the incomplete monumentality of the KNSM-laan for all. The avenue, however, is not strong enough to unite the individual buildings. The rear-side character of the strip of buildings north of the avenue is just as inauspicious as the avenue's terminating in the rather disappointing apartment building by Jo Coenen, which has none of the monumental effect it suggested in model form. Nor is this peninsula well served by the fact that at the street level, the image of both Wiel Arets' tower and the Quist Wintermans blocks, with maisonnettes of one and a half levels along a central corridor, is defined by the parking facilities. Moreover, Arets' abstract tower has sadly lost a great deal of its effect in less than 10 years, because the black on some concrete façade panels has discoloured faster than on others, negating the powerfully suggested monolithic quality to a great extent.

As a whole, the KNSM Island is no great success, although Piraeus by Hans Kollhoff and Christian Rapp is one of the most unique buildings in the entire Eastern Harbour District. Since its completion, it has become the reference point and testing standard for just about every large residential building in the Netherlands. The last project on the KNSM Island, on either side of the spot where the Verbindingsdam touches land, is the two-part apartment building by Diener & Diener, which joins in the competition for rigour waged by Piraeus and Arets' tower. The more interesting of these two building sections by Diener & Diener is the smaller block, the Hofhaus, because of its unique housing typology, in which the usual hierarchy in the size of the rooms is absent.

The project by Diener & Diener forms the link between the KNSM and Java, which in many ways is the least fussy islands of the Eastern Harbour District. The architecture along the little canals, and certainly the bridges over those canals, might suffer from an overdose of free expression, but the majority of the island consists of large subdued apartment buildings without too much demonstrative typological or architectural experimentation fever. None of the architects involved seems to have wanted or been able to outshine the others. This results in a strong unity among the blocks by Sjoerd Soeters, Jo Crépain, Christiaanse, Cruz & Ortiz, Uytenhaak, Karelse Van der Meer, Cees Nagelkerke, Bob van Reeths, Architectenwerkgroep (AWG), Geurst & Schulze, Baneke Van der Hoeven and Meyer en Van Schooten. Despite the sometimes considerable variations in colour and façade treatment, the blocks sustain and understand one another. A few simple guidelines, such as a mandated flat dock façade without protruding elements, proved an effective way to create peace and order.

The apartment buildings, with for each entrance hall a lift that goes down to the parking garages under the raised inner court-yards, offer democratic comfort. Public-sector and private-sector rental units and owner-occupied dwellings are set side by side, with a view onto the IJ or the IJhaven for virtually all the dwellings, and a balcony, terrace or conservatory on the southwest side. The Java Island includes a range of housing types within the large apartment buildings, attuned to various target groups, from simple studios and two-room flats to large apartments and maisonnettes, all of which fit within the same pattern featuring a façade 5.4 metres wide.

There was no quest for revolutionary innovation on the Java Island. Instead the known typologies were recycled in an inventive way, and the familiar premise that the dwelling is the material from which the city is built was maintained. This resulted in a residential environment with the potential for the same timeless quality as the housing in Plan-Zuid. which was based on similar principles. What might most hamper that timeless quality is the sometimes all too basic detailing of the architecture; the entrances in particular have little allure. It needed not be as opulent as the entrance of Piraeus, the most beautiful of the entire Eastern Harbour District, but on Java they were all executed somewhat on the frugal side, for which the generous dimensions cannot compentate.

Whereas a simple balance was found between the individualism of the apartment and the collective spaces within the blocks on the Java Island, on Borneo and Sporenburg housing has been privatized to an almost neurotic degree, and the street has been deliberately designed as a no man's land. Streets and docks have been designed as a rest area open to the public between the introverted patio dwellings. Rigid guidelines on the height of the ground floor, the use of materials and colours, the positioning of the dwellings back to back and the mandate that parking had to be addressed within the contours of the block created a straitjacket within which the designer and the resident were granted relatively little room to manoeuvre. It is true that surprising spatial variations did manage to emerge within this straitjacket, but in most cases this still amounted to a variant of the traditional drive-in dwelling, with a carport and one room on the ground floor, the main living quarters on the level above, and on top of that half a level for sleeping quarters and a roof terrace.

These restrictive guidelines result in restrictive dwellings, which are suitable for only one type of use. The ranks of rooms on the street level in the block on the Stuurmankade, by Van Gameren and Mastenbroek of de Architectengroep, illustrate this. Almost all the residents use the space on the ground floor as home offices, places in which to work. The arrangement of this room is highly similar in every dwelling, mostly with a desk with a computer across the front wall, a bookcase against the rear wall and a comfortable chair in the remaining space. The bookcase also seems to be filled to a large extent with more or less the same books, which gives a good indication of the social monoculture that has arisen here.

The back-to-back patio home, in this form and definitely
with such narrow façades, has all sorts of limitation on use.
The layout, with a level for living quarters and two bedrooms,
usually split between the ground level and the roof level, puts a
limit on the size of families. Closing off the carport and building
a roof extension are costly escapes for the space shortage
that comes with family expansion, but even then they remain
dwellings free of much excess. Here the designers were
often given a little more slack. They break the monotony of the
endless row of closed façades, which make Borneo and
Sporenburg an especially photogenic neighbourhood but
make for a less than ideal housing environment in some ways .
Aside from their limited dimensions, half of the dwellings are
almost entirely oriented to the north, and an equal percentage
are situated on a narrow inner street and lack any view onto
the water, which is after all one of the charms of the Eastern
Harbour District. The streets themselves are laid out in a
spartan style, and this emphasizes the hard division between
home and street, which the residents do not always accept.
Slow-motion green guerrilla warfare has been waged for
years, in which the residents are trying to take over the streets
bit by bit.

The strict guidelines have certainly minimized the potential
for architectural expression on Sporenburg, and without
wishing to do anyone an injustice, the result is that the façades
are to a large extent interchangeable. On Borneo the stage
management has been somewhat less strictly imposed. This is
where we find projects that manage to deviate the most from
the more less mandated standard of back-to-back housing.
This also applies to the unique head ends, with lateral housing
units by Van Gameren and Mastenbroek and by Miralles and
Tagliabue, and it applies for instance for the project by Uytenhaak, which weaves dwellings together in a Gordian knot and
has them extending into the façade width of their neighbours.
Van Herk & De Kleijn were the only ones who managed to really
break free of the back-to-back solution and create dwellings
with two-sided orientations, giving everyone views and light.
They even managed to let the sunlight penetrate to the north
side of the block.

Finally, the Rietlanden, out of the six neighbourhoods in the
Eastern Harbour District, is most like a frayed edge. It is not
so much an area with a character fully its own, like Sporenburg

and Java, but rather a collection site for colliding directions.
The block structure that begins at the Veemarkt and the
Abattoir stops abruptly here. The sea of low-rises of Sporenburg, which continues as far as the black-hued blocks by
Claus en Kaan, also terminates here. The existing buildings
along the Oostelijke Handelskade are absorbed, and the
different flows from the Panamalaan, Piet Hein Tunnel and
Piet Heinkade merge here. The free-standing blocks of offices
by Hans van Heeswijk and dwellings by Venhoeven C.S.,
through their free parcel allotment and autonomous form,
are an adequate and logical way to fill in this difficult area.
Venhoeven's inflated aluminium block also gives this unavoid-
ably untidy neighbourhood a face recognizable from afar.

Architectural criticism usually limits itself to a critique of the
building around the completion date. Most of the buildings
in the Eastern Harbour District have been up long enough to
allow for discussion of the experience of daily use as well,
which in my case, as a resident of the Java Island, is a personal
experience. Aside from the unmistakable satisfaction of living
in an environment that was designed with so much care and
attention for architectural and urban-planning quality, as a
resident I also experience the odd dualism that characterizes
this area: in terms of density, appearance and location right
next to the centre of Amsterdam, it is urban, yet at the same
time, because housing almost entirely dominates, it is simply
a suburb. The neighbourhood shopping centre, the eating and
drinking establishments scattered around the area, the schools
and the mini-version of a furniture mart in Loods 6 on KNSM
do little to alter that. The Eastern Harbour District, like all
suburbs in the Netherlands, is inhabited by the working middle
class. This means a suburban quiet reigns here on weekdays
between nine and five o'clock, which even the steadily
increasing number of children in the area does little to disturb
so far. So it is a blessing that, for years, hardly a day has gone
by without some architecture tourism. Strolling and cycling
around, these tourists at least bring some life to the area.

Borneo and Sporenburg

View of the Borneokade, around 1910

eo and Sporenburg, 1980s Borneo and Sporenburg, 1980s

Borneo and Sporenburg under construction, 1990s

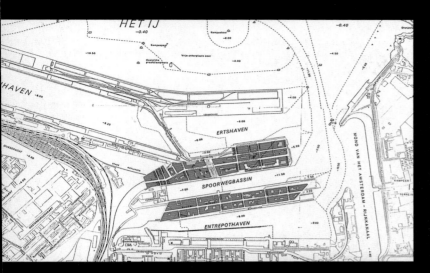

ic urban-planning principles, 1992

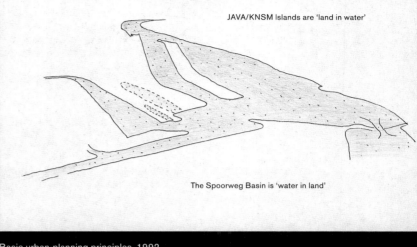

JAVA/KNSM Islands are 'land in water'

The Spoorweg Basin is 'water in land'

Basic urban-planning principles, 1992

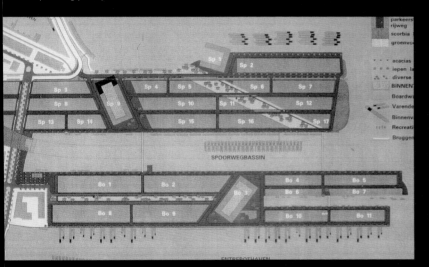

of the public space, 1995

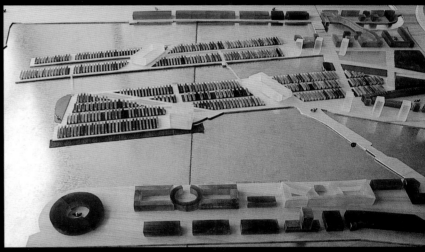

Urban plan West 8, 1998

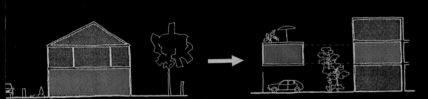

dard Dutch low rise   Borneo Sporenburg typology

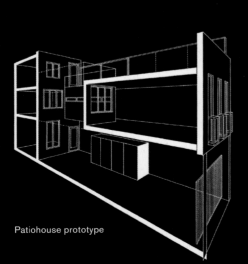

Patiohouse prototype

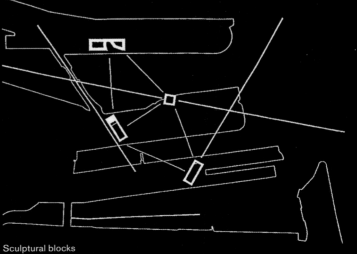

Sculptural blocks

View of the Ertskade from the Levantkade

View of the J.F. van Hengelstraat from the Levantkade

View of the J.F. van Hengelstraat from the Levantkade

View of the Stuurmankade from the C. van Eesterenlaan

Borneo and Sporenburg
Marlies Buurman

The peninsulas Borneo and Sporenburg were built up between 1996 and 2000 with a large number of low-rise dwellings in a high density of 100 housing units per hectare and several large blocks. The urban-planning structure selected deviates from that of the previous district sections. An extensive study preceded this.

The Policy Document on Basic Principles in 1989 proposed considering the two islands on either side of the narrowest harbour basin, the Spoorweg basin, as one area and developing them together. In keeping with this the Spoorweg basin was seen as a 'water plaza', a connecting element instead of a barrier.

Development began in 1992, and the Easter Harbour District project group decided that about 2150 dwellings should be built, distributed over the two

sector. New Deal, a collective of corporations, signed on and decided to take on the development of the housing. New Deal obtained permission from the city to develop an urban plan and build a large proportion of the dwellings. In addition, the collective was allowed to build the dwellings and facilities under a full profit- and risk-scheme. New Deal set out the basic principles of urban planning in association with the Spatial Planning Department (Dienst Ruimtelijke Ordening, or DRO). Because the dwellings on Borneo-Sporenburg would come on the market at the same time as those on the Java Island, a distinctive housing offering seemed desirable, and low-rise dwellings for families with children, as well as houses with individual front front doors on the street, were chosen. The choice of low-rise construction was also underscored from an urban-planning point of view – giving the area its own kind of building construction amid the high-rises of the surrounding islands would be beneficial for the orientation and the recognizability of

View of the head of the Borneo Island from the Zuiderijdijk

View of the head of the Sporenburg Island from the Zuiderijdijk

Because fitting 100 housing units per hectare in low-rise buildings was a very difficult challenge, the plan that Rudy Uytenhaak had devised earlier for the Java Island was looked at again. This study showed that if the dwellings were stacked in a compact construction of parcels on narrow streets, the high density was feasible. The challenge was then presented to six architecture firms –Rudy Uytenhaak, Claus en Kaan, Van Berkel & Bos, Heren 5, Holvast and Van Woerden, and Liesbeth van der Pol. These firms submitted very divergent plans, which in any event confirmed that it was possible, with a building height of three to four levels, to achieve a varied neighbourhood with the required density. This did imply that a large proportion of the dwellings would have to be built back to back.

In 1993 the firms of Wytze Patijn, Quadrat and West 8 were asked to provide an urban-planning vision for the two islands based on the previously formulated basic principles and the insights gained along the way. Patijn based his design on the view and the space and designed a park landscape

in which the dwellings were housed in large residential blocks after all. In Quadrat's plan, the public space was seen as a regulating element and the Spoorweg basin served as a central water plaza. The various transport flows were each given their own positions – cars low and the slower traffic high. This plan did not meet the requirements either and was too complex. The plan by Adriaan Geuze of West 8 was the only one to combine all the basic principles. Geuze housed all the ground-connected dwellings in 'slats' – strips four metres wide and 35 metres deep and three levels in height. These slats alternated with open strips of the same dimensions. This created a tightly ordered repetition of introverted low-rise dwellings. The plan was refined with help from Rudy Uytenhaak and implemented.

The area has since become characterized by long rows of back-to-back dwellings with patios or roof terraces. This has produced dwellings oriented inward with a great deal of privacy. Vital to the streetscape is that every house has its own front door on the street and that the streets have narrow

View of the Stuurmankade from the Panamakade

View of the Panamakade from the Stuurmankade

dimensions. The result is a sharp contrast between the enclosed quality of the dwellings and the streets and the wide-open vistas onto the IJ.

The elaboration of the dwellings was entrusted to more than 30 architects, who designed a large number of patio-dwelling types with flexible layouts, based on a prototype. Most dwellings have a ground floor 3.5 metres high, which provides room for split-levels and galleries. Moreover, this lets daylight penetrate deep into the dwelling. In most dwellings the sitting room is located on the upper floor, which sharpens the division between the public and the private space. The materials, selected in advance, mainly dark-red brick, western red cedar and hinged gates, provide cohesion in the residential area.

The preconditions stipulated by West 8 compelled the architects to be as creative as possible. The results can be found mainly behind the façades, but in a few instances they can also be seen on the exterior, such as the wedge-shaped dwellings by Van Herk & de Kleijn, the alternating built-up and vacant parcels by M3H (following the basic design by Geuze) and the houses by

Neutelings Riedijk Architecten, with their protruding boxes of cedarwood that provide a view onto the street. All the dwellings on the island heads are turned a quarter-turn in relation to the prevailing building orientation and stand out by their use of materials. Josep Lluís Mateo clad the so-called 'panorama dwellings' in tropical hardwood, and Mastenbroek and Van Gameren fitted their head dwellings with projecting, covered terraces clad in glass of various colours.

Three large residential buildings were located amidst the many low-rise dwellings. Geuze dubbed them 'meteorites', as though they had crashed here, but in fact they were very carefully positioned in sightlines to significant points in the surroundings. Pacman, by Koen van Velsen, for example, is positioned in a line with the Oranjesluizen locks, the silver-coloured The Whale, by Frits van Dongen, in a line with the Verbindingsdam (Connecting Dam) and the third monolith, Fountainhead, by Kees Christiaanse, is to stand in the sight axis of the east on-ramp of the Piet Hein Tunnel. Fountainhead was

View of the heads of Borneo and Sporenburg from the Zuiderijdijk

designed as a cube of 60 by 60 metres and is supposed to be positioned halfway in the water on the Ertskade on Sporenburg. It is unlikely that the plan will be implemented, but if the building is built, it will be related to the other 60-metre towers in the district that present themselves as landmarks when viewed from the A10 ring motorway (the IJ Tower by Neutelings Riedijk Architecten in the Rietlanden and the Water Tower by Atelier PRO in Entrepot-West). Due in part to these meteorites, the intented housing density has been achieved.

Geuze's urban plan also had a significant influence on the plan by the DRO for the public space. The compact plan allows hardly any green amenities. However, the surrounding water is seen as a compensatory element – the designers treat the 'blue' as green. One exception is the diagonal strip of greenery on Sporenburg, the carefully planned location of which provides spectacular through-views onto the water and the other islands from either side. In addition, the layout is sober and is characterized by the use of broad,

high kerbs and a single type of brick for all carriageways and parking spaces. Only the dock plaza on the head of Sporenburg deviates from this with its paving of scoria bricks.

The eye-catching elements in the area are the two brigh-red bridges by West 8 spanning the 90-metre-wide Spoorweg basin between the two peninsulas. The western bridge is used by cyclists and pedestrians, while the eastern bridge, with its high curve, is used only by pedestrians. At its highest point, it is as high as the buildings surrounding it and provides a fantastic view onto the water and the neighbourhood. The curved balustrades are noteworthy, as are the swaying lamps, which are reminiscent of birds' heads. A third, more sober bridge spans the entrance harbour on Borneo.

View of the Stuurmankade

View of the Stuurmankade

Scheepstimmermanstraat

On the north side of a former inner harbour on the Borneo peninsula, a unique experiment was carried out. Here, 60 parcels were alloted to buyers who, in association with an architect each could select from among a list of candidates, were allowed to build their ideal house. These dream houses had to be built within strict specifications as well. The parcels are 16 metres deep and vary in width from 4.2 to 6 metres. The maximum height of the houses is 9.2 metres and the ground floor had to be 3.5 metres. These are spacious houses. Some surface areas reach 400 m².

The access to the houses is on the Scheepstimmermanstraat; to the rear, the houses are lined directly on the water of the inner harbour. The floor plans of most houses are oriented to the rear, because of the location on the water and orientation to the south. This varied strip of houses can best be viewed from the other side of the entrance harbour. What stands out is not just the alternating use of materials, but also the fact that almost all the façades open onto the water with large windows, some with folding wooden shutters or rusty louvered panels, and that the narrow parcels are put to maximum use. The opposite can also be seen. Some architects and clients attached great value to the garden on the water, which in some cases resulted in a lot of space being sacrificed inside. The result is often nothing more than an uncomfortable-looking little garden or patio, wedged in between high walls.

The façades on the street side have a more closed character and often literally serve as screens, such as the houses by Faro and Koen van Velsen. As in the rest of the area, cars had to be parked inside. In several places, two cars can be parked on the parcel thanks to a mechanical system. In other places, simple inclines have been used. This did not always result in very neat solutions, but a few cases, such as the house by MVRDV at number 26, proves that it is possible. The painstaking finish of the grey-stucco incline means the parking space is a pleasant sight even when the car is not parked there.

View of the Stuurmankade from the Panamakade

Canal between the Scheepstimmermanstraat and the Stokerkade

The Scheepstimmermanstraat can be seen as a reflection of the prevailing
ideas on public housing in the 1990s, determined in large part by the housing
wishes of the housing consumer. The experiment has been deemed a success
by the commissioning clients and the city and will be repeated on the IJburg
archipelago in the IJmeer lake.

or 1   architecture firm **West 8 Urban Design & Landscape Architecture**   project architect **Adriaan Geuze, Daniel Janslin, Rudolf Eilander**   project **Sister bridges**   programme **bicycle and pedestrian bridges**   client **Ingenieursbureau Amsterdam**   completion **2000**

26/27 architecture firm **among others, Ruimtelab, MVRDV, Christian Rapp, de Architectengroep, Heren 5 Architecten, Faro Architecten, Gunnar Daan** project **60 freehold parcels**
programme **60 dwellings** client **private individuals** design/completion **1996/2000**

142

26-16/18 architecture firm **Ruimtelab** project architect **René Heijne, Jacques Vink** project **double residence** programme **2 dwellings (private sector)** client **H. Houtman, H. Radema** design/completion **1998/2000**

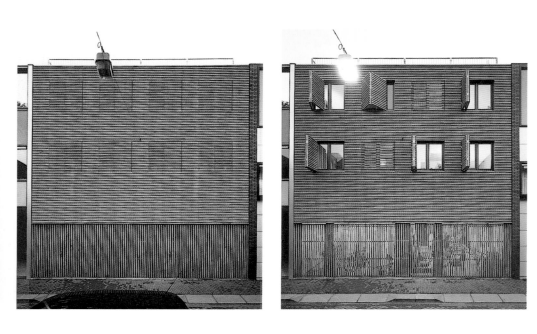

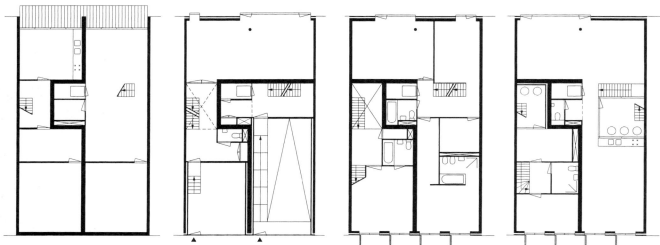

26-22 architecture firm **INBO Architecten** project architect **Hans Toornstra** project **dwelling on the Scheepstimmermanstraat** programme **1 dwelling (private sector)** client **M.J. de Nijs en Zonen construction company, Warmenhuizen** design/completion **1998/2000**

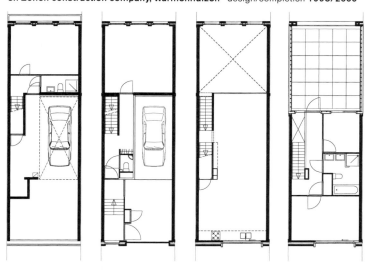

26 -2/4 architecture firm **Tekton Architekten** project architect **Bert Tjhie** project **Soetira** programme **work-at-home dwelling (private sector)** client **I.M. Coopman**
design/completion **1997/2003**

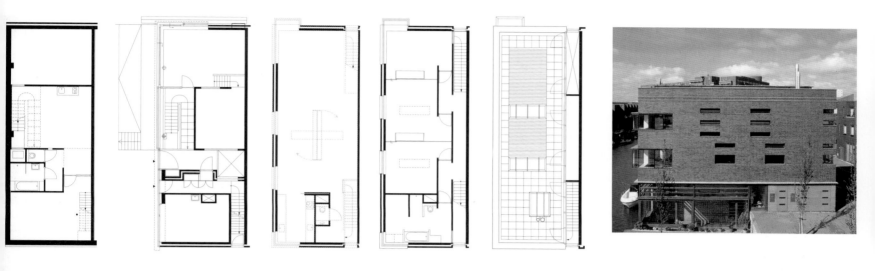

27 -80/82 architecture firm **Heren 5 Architecten** project architect **Ed Bijman, Jan Klomp, Bas Liesker, Dirk van Gestel** project **Parcel 37, ground- and first-floor dwelling**
programme **private dwellings (private sector)** client **City Centre Department, Amsterdam** design/completion **1997/2000**

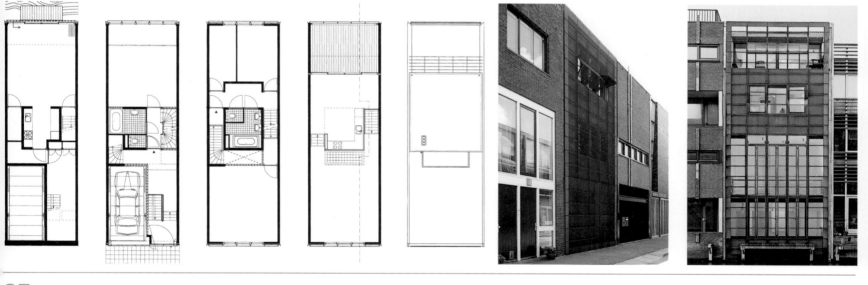

27 -100 architecture firm **INBO Architecten** project architect **Jan Hoedemaker** project **Neyman House** programme **1 dwelling (private sector)** client **M.J. de Nijs en Zonen construction
company, Warmenhuizen** design/completion **1998/2000**

27-110 architecture firm **Heren 5 Architecten** project architect **Ed Bijman, Jan Klomp, Bas Liesker, Dirk van Gestel** project **Parcel 49** programme **private residence** client **Mr Van Duynhoven, F.J. Pleur** design/completion **1997/2000**

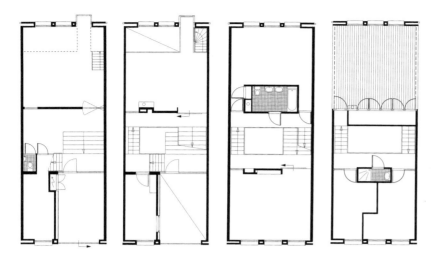

27-120 architecture firm **Architectenbureau K. van Velsen** project architect **Koen van Velsen** project **Vos House** programme **1 dwelling (freehold parcel)** client **L.A.B. Vos** design/completion **1997/1999**

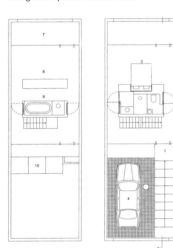

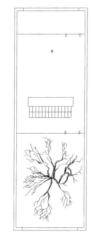

27-126 architecture firm **Architectuurstudio Herman Hertzberger** project architect **Herman Hertzberger, Henk de Weijer, Dickens van der Werff, Cor Kruter** project **dwelling on Borneo Island** programme **1 dwelling (private sector)** client **F.C. Schirmeister** design/completion **1996/1999**

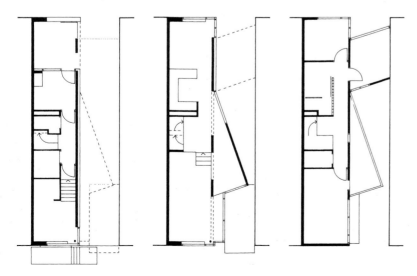

18 architecture firm **Architectenbureau K. van Velsen** project architect **Koen van Velsen** project **Pacman** programme **207 dwellings (private sector), commercial space, garage**
client **Stichting Pensioenfonds voor de Bouwnijverheid (construction industry pension fund)** design/completion **1994/1997**

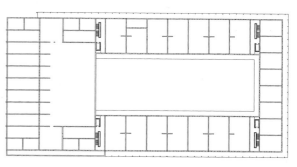

fourth floor

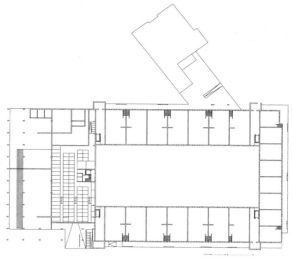

ground floor

17 architecture firm **Heren 5 Architecten**   project architect **Ed Bijman, Jan Klomp, Bas Liesker, Dirk van Gestel, Jacobien Hofstede, Alissa Labeur**   project **BO9**   programme **dwellings (private sector and public-sector rental)**   client **New Deal development company, Amsterdam**   design/completion **1999/2001**

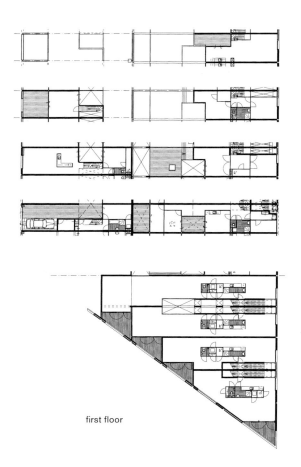

first floor

25 architecture firm **MAP Architects** project architect **Josep Lluis Mateo** project **Borneo Island housing construction** programme **26 units** client **M.J. de Nijs en Zonen construction** company, **Warmenhuizen** design/completion **1995/2000**

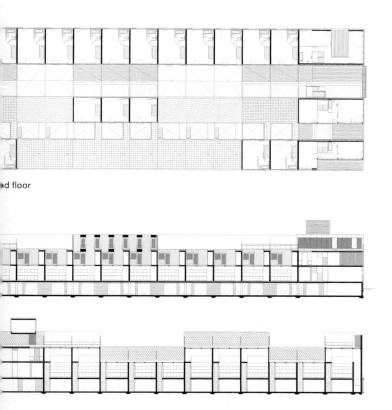

d floor

73 architecture firm **Heren 5 Architecten** project architect **Ed Bijman, Jan Klomp, Bas Liesker** project **SP4** programme **dwellings (private sector)** client **New Deal development company,** **Amsterdam** design/completion **1997/2000**

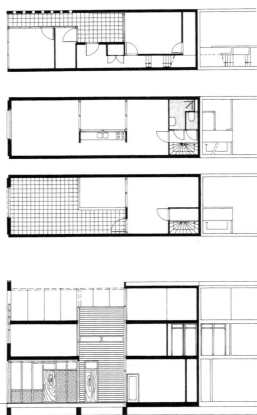

31   architecture firm **KCAP**   project architect **Han van den Born**   project **Borneo**   programme **44 ground-linked houses, built-in garage**   client **Smits construction company, Beverwijk**
design/completion **1994/1998**

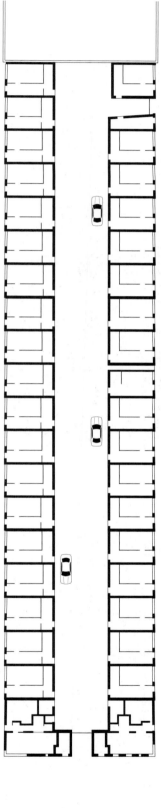

58/80   architecture firm **M3H architecten**   project architect **M. Reniers, M. Spaan, M. Henssen, H. Hammink**   project **SP7 and SP8**   programme **dwellings (public-sector rental)**
client **New Deal development company, Amsterdam**   design/completion **1994/2000**

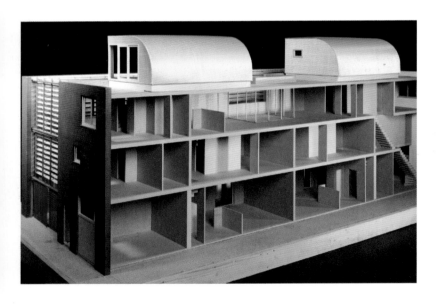

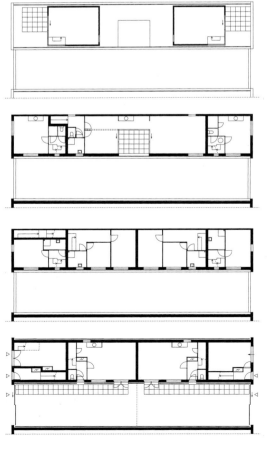

46/56/68 architecture firm **Claus en Kaan Architecten** project architect **Felix Claus, Kees Kaan** project **Sporenburg** programme **dwellings (private sector and public-sector rental)** client **New Deal development company, Amsterdam** design/completion **1994/2000**

70 architecture firm **Steven Holl Architects** project architect **Justin Vorhammer** project **Fountainhead** programme **97 loft apartments, 229 parking spaces, restaurant, fitness centre, sauna, swimming pool, studio, workspace, office** client **New Deal development company, Amsterdam** design/completion **1994/not realized**

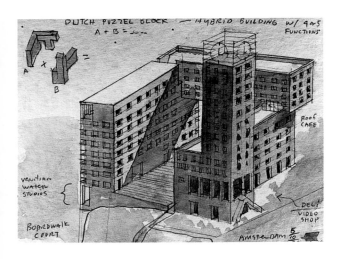

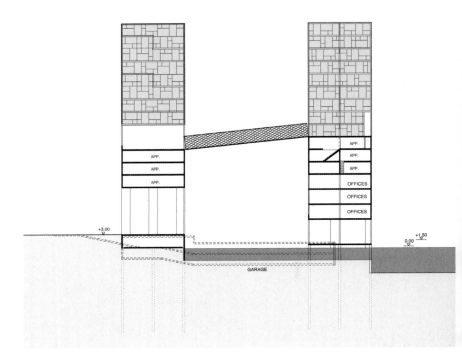

70 architecture firm **KCAP** project architect **Kees Christiaanse, Irma van Oort** project **Fountainhead** programme **97 loft apartments, 229 parking spaces, restaurant, fitness centre, sauna, swimming pool, studio, workspace, office** client **New Deal development, Amsterdam** design/completion **1999/not realized**

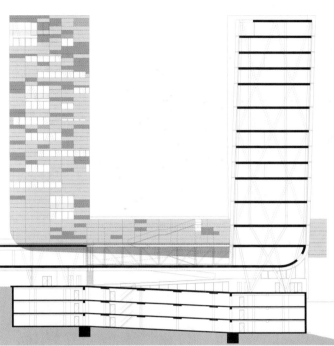

64 / 65   architecture firm **Neutelings Riedijk Architecten**   project architect **Willem Jan Neutelings, Michiel Riedijk**   project **Sporenburg**   programme **5 villas and 27 dwellings with 9 commercial spaces**   client **New Deal development company, Amsterdam**   design/completion **1994/1999**

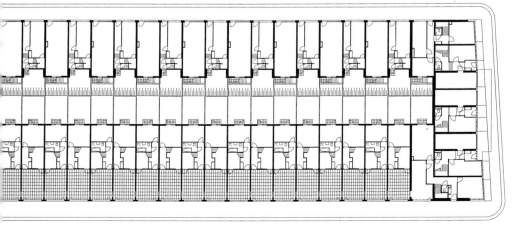

ground floor

49 / 55 / 63 architecture firm **DKV architekten** project architect **Dolf Dobbelaar, Herman de Kovel, Paul de Vroom** project **urban dwellings on the IJ on Borneo-Sporenburg**

programme **12 six-room dwellings, 18 five-room dwellings, 28 four-room dwellings, 15 three-room dwellings, commercial space** client **New Deal development company, Amsterdam**

design/completion **1994/1997**

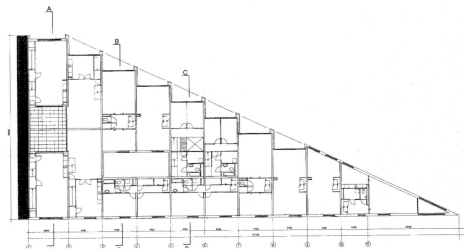

first floor

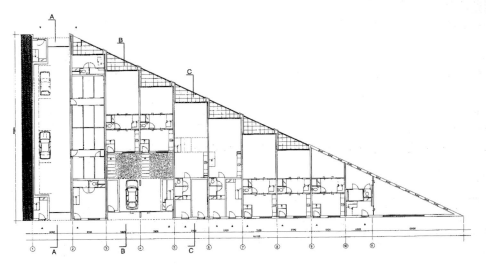

ground floor

28 architecture firm **de Architectengroep** project architect **Dick van Gameren, Bjarne Mastenbroek** project **Borneo Island dwellings** programme **58 dwellings (private sector)** client **Smits construction company, Beverwijk** design/completion **1996/1999**

second floor

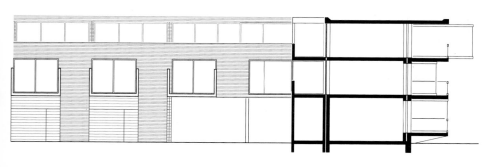

29 / 30   architecture firm **Enric Miralles**   project architect **Enric Miralles, Benedetta Tagliabue**   project **Borneo Island dwellings**   programme **6 dwellings**   client **private commission**
design/completion **1996/2000**

72 / 74   architecture firm **Van Sambeek en Van Veen Architecten**   project architect **Erna van Sambeek**   project **SP6/7 and SP4**   programme **24 and 30 dwellings (private sector)**
client **New Deal development company, Amsterdam**   design/completion **1994/1999**

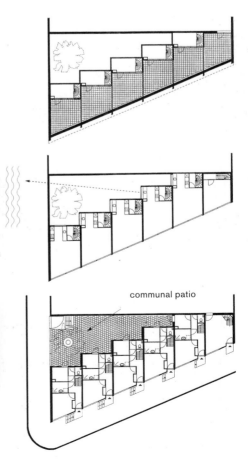

communal patio

44 / 76   architecture firm **Atelier Zeinstra van der Pol**   project architect **Herman Zeinstra**   project **Sporenburg**   programme **83 public-sector rental and 16 private-sector dwellings**
client **New Deal development company, Amsterdam**   design/completion **1994/1999**

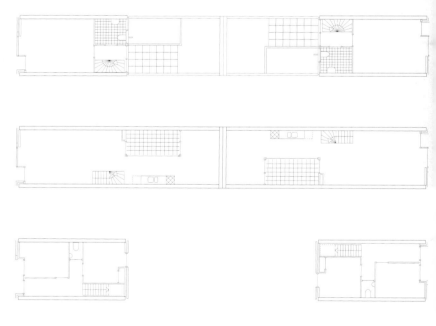

22 architecture firm **Atelier Zeinstra van der Pol** project architect **Liesbeth van der Pol** project **Borneo** programme **50 rental dwellings (private sector)** client **SFB Vastgoed/BPF Bouw, Amsterdam** design/completion **1994/1999**

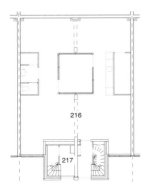

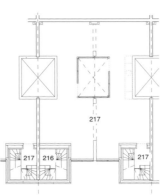

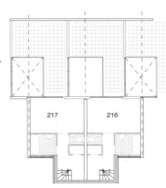

36 architecture firm **Architectenbureau Marlies Rohmer** project architect **Marlies Rohmer** project **Borneo Island housing construction** programme **67 single-family dwellings, 21 of which as studio-dwellings (public-sector rental), parking garage** client **New Deal development company, Amsterdam** design/completion **1997/2000**

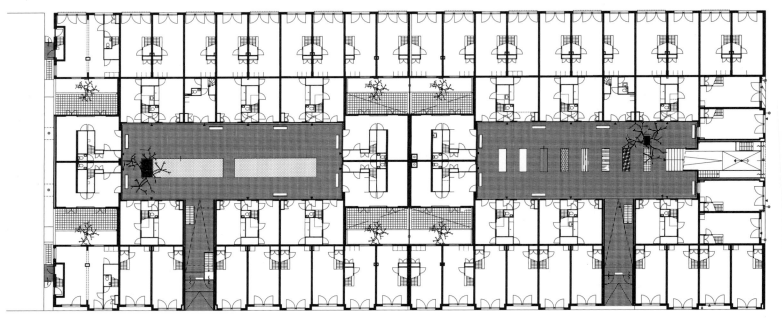

ground floor

42 architecture firm **de Architecten Cie.** project architect **Frits van Dongen** project **The Whale** programme **150 public-sector rental dwellings, 64 private-sector rental dwellings, 1100 m² of commercial space, 179 parking spaces** client **New Deal development company, Amsterdam** design/completion **1995/2001**

oor

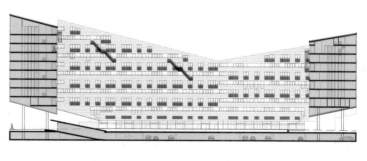

floor

42

40 architecture firm **Köther & Salman Architekten** project architect **Köther & Salman Architekten** project **SP2 and SP14** programme **SP2: 24 dwellings; SP14: 34 dwellings** client **New Deal development company, Amsterdam** design/completion **1994/1999**

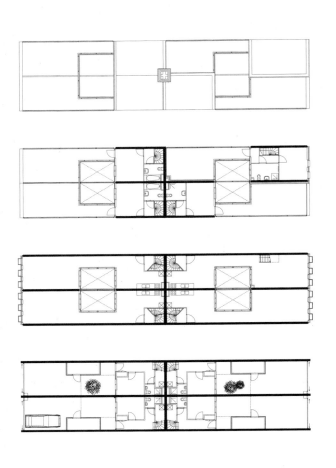

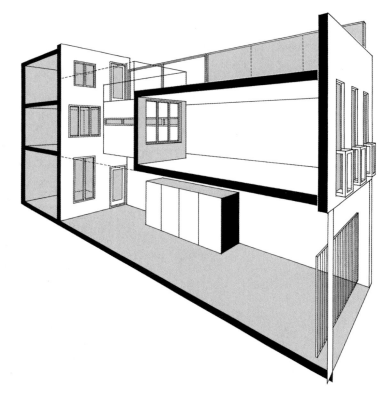

51 architecture firm **Ruimtelab** project architect **René Heijne, Jacques Vink** project **panoramadwellings** programme **5 dwellings (private sector)** client **New Deal development company, Amsterdam** design/completion **1997/1999**

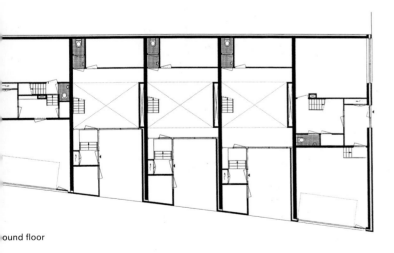

ound floor

59 architecture firm **Heren 5 Architecten** project architect **Ed Bijman, Jan Klomp, Bas Liesker** project **SP7** programme **dwellings (private sector)** client **New Deal development company, Amsterdam** design/completion **1996/1999**

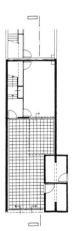

24 architecture firm **Van Herk & De Kleijn architecten**   project architect **Arne van Herk**   project **Borneo Island dwellings**   programme **28 owner-occupied dwellings (private sector),** built-in garage (28 cars)   client **M.J. de Nijs en Zonen construction company, Warmenhuizen**   design/completion **1994/1999**

second floor

15/16 architecture firm **Rudy Uytenhaak architectenbureau**   project architect **R. Uytenhaak, E. van der Zaag, J. Zondag**   project **Patio Malaparte**   programme **36 dwellings** **(private sector), 90 dwellings (public-sector rental)**   client **New Deal development company, Amsterdam**   design/completion **1996/2000**

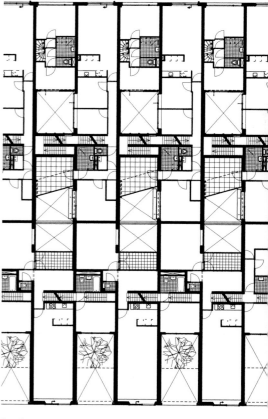

first floor

Pure infrastructure

Ed Melet

Ports are pure infrastructure. They are laid out for the express purpose of making the transfer of goods to and from ships as smooth as possible. The Eastern Harbour District of Amsterdam was just such a pragmatic area. The various islands built in the IJ starting in the late nineteenth century consisted of docks, a lot of railroad tracks and some hangars. Nothing more. Everything was geared toward an efficient handling of goods, but the harbours were poorly accessible from the city centre. Only trains could easily reach the harbour islands. Not that this was all that surprising. This way, the negative side-effects of the port and its activities, noise and stench, could, to a certain extent, remain confined to this isolated area.

However, when port activities began a steady exodus from the Eastern Harbour District to the western harbours – closer to the North Sea, of much more ambitious proportions and better connected to the road network – this isolated location proved a liability. They became a deserted, unsupervised area.

Bridge or tunnel

When the city considered new functions for this area in the late 1970s, one of the pre-eminent issues was how the Eastern Harbour District was to be made accessible. The various plans provide a good picture of how views on the absorption of the area within the city developed.

It was quickly apparent that an IJ Boulevard had to be built. This avenue, along which it was initially thought that companies with international operations would open premises, was meant not only to link the city centre to the Eastern Harbour District, but also to provide a connection to IJburg, a new city district planned for the western section of the IJmeer lake, which was to house no fewer than 100,000 inhabitants. Therefore a wide, four-lane carriageway with a metro line underneath, both of which would cross the Amsterdam-Rijnkanaal waterway via a bridge 10 metres high, seemed an obvious choice initially.

As is usually the case in this sort of large-scale project, reality changed faster than the planning. For instance, business concerns like ABN-AMRO and ING decided to open premises not along the banks of the IJ, but in the Zuidas (South Axis) area closer to Schiphol Airport, forcing the city to adjust its programme. However, sometimes reality did not change fast enough. This is most clearly illustrated by the development of the Piet Hein Tunnel.

This tunnel under the Amsterdam-Rijnkanaal was conceived by the city's Spatial Planning Department (Dienst Ruimtelijke Ordening, or DRO) to replace the original plan's bridge – a costly but logical adjustment. The bridge over the channel would have necessitated a wide carriageway, right through the middle of the area. With the intensive use anticipated, this would entail a huge noise and environmental toll and necessitate putting up noise barriers. This would mean not only the loss of valuable land, but also the end of the harbours' inherent character. This latter aspect was not a major concern for the city at the time. In its plan, the harbour basins were to be filled in and partially laid out as parks. The greenbelt areas thus created would compensate for the high density (100 housing units per hectare) planned for housing construction on the islands.

The new plan, including the tunnel, took far greater advantage of the unique nature of this area and had as its premise that the surrounding water provided more than ample compensation for the high-density construction. To that end, the new residential areas would have to be designed so that they derived maximum benefit from their surroundings. Noise barriers that would hinder the view did not fit into this picture. This vision eventually won out.

Special

The Piet Hein Tunnel is one and a half kilometres long, lies on the bottom of the Spoorweg basin and the Amsterdam-Rijnkanaal and, among other things, assures the Eastern Harbour District a rapid connection to the A10 motorway. The tunnel is constructed out of caissons manufactured in Belgium and shipped to this location by way of the North Sea and the IJ. This kind of tunnel has of course been built before – although this is, to date, the longest in the Netherlands – but its construction was nevertheless a challenge of epic proportions. The concrete tunnel elements being shipped in was a spectacular sight. The tops of the tunnel fragments were visible above the water line like the backs of whales. One by one, the elements of the tunnel shaft were sunk in a extremely precise process. They were coupled together with rubber seals which the water pressure compressed to such a degree that they made the tunnel waterproof. Just to be on the safe side, the seams were lined on the inside with an omega seal. In actuality, three tunnels were built in this way: two for automobile traffic, each with two lanes, and south of that, the tunnel shaft for the IJtram, the public transport connection between IJburg and the Central Station.

Whereas most tunnels vanish entirely into the ground and lead a more or less anonymous existence, the entrance to the Piet Hein Tunnel was made into a special element. With its four percent incline, it rises slowly out of the Spoorweg basin to a point six metres above the Amsterdam ordnance level, affording a view of the Amsterdam city centre – from a playground built on the roof. Of course, the tunnel was not extended onto land and thus made longer than strictly necessary simply in order to create a special site. The major advantage is that traffic does not emerge from the tunnel until halfway into the Rietlanden and only then creates any noise nuisance. This would create an additional noise-abatement zone between Sporenburg and Borneo, allowing the extension of the streets in West 8's urban plan up to that point.

The IJtram provides a rapid connection between IJburg and the Central Station. It covers the 8.5 kilometres in 18 minutes, one and half times as fast as an ordinary tram. The IJtram was originally conceived as a metro. However, plans for IJburg changed; far fewer people would be living there. This change from metro to tram entailed some logistical problems. The tunnel shaft for the metro was laid on the south side of the automobile tunnels. This makes little difference for a metro, since it moves more or less independently of all other traffic. However, a tram rides above ground, and the route to Central Station meant that the tram line and the automobile carriageway would have to cross each other immediately after leaving the tunnel. An even more complicated intersection, difficult to get across, would have been the result. Therefore the city decided to run the tram line under the carriageway. The underground tram comes into view at the Rietlanden stop. Like the metro station originally planned, this stop lies deep below the ground surface – but in a trench, hence in the open air. In an effort to increase public safety, the granite-lined walls of this excavated stop are set at an angle. From the surrounding buildings, what goes on six metres below the surface is clearly visible.

Cars

Besides the change from a metro line to a tram line, the route for automobile traffic was also significantly altered. Upon closer study, the broad IJ Boulevard initially conceived, with the expected stream of cars into the already crowded city centre, turned out to be undesirable. So a new section of the ring road was conceived in order to make the centre accessible. Via the Panamaweg, traffic from the Piet Hein Tunnel emerges onto this ring and then onto the existing ring – the Mauritskade and the Stadhouderskade. Traffic can also drive up the Piet Hein-kade or reach the KNSM Island via a small detour.

This latter route is the result of an adjustment, not very surprising in itself, in the DRO's plan. This originally envisioned the Panamalaan running in a straight line via a new bridge all the way to the point at which the KNSM and Java Islands merge. However, another bridge, so close to the connecting dam that had provided access for the KNSM Island ever since the construction of the islands, seemed superfluous. In addition, the residents who had squatted the buildings at the spot where the bridge would touch land had major objections. In order to avoid excessive delays to the project's progress, and because the bridge seemed not to contribute very much to efficient access for the islands, the residents got what they wanted: the bridge was scrapped.

The IJtram, the extension of tram line 10 to the Java and KNSM Islands and the complex intersection where traffic now merges from three directions (Piet Hein Tunnel, Panamakanaal, KNSM Island) all served to form a traffic knot in the Rietlanden that would be tricky to untangle. Originally, the plan was for the surrounding residential neighbourhoods to logically extend into the Rietlanden. The traffic noise, however, made any sort of high-density construction in this area impossible, or in any event very expensive. Moreover, space had to be created for a safe and well-ordered site for the various traffic flows. Hence the Rietlanden area has been turned into one large park, made up of grass-covered 'floes'. These soften the visual impact of the traffic to a certain extent. A large number of Italian poplar trees is also meant to muffle the traffic noise.

Steel bridges

Although the bridge from the Panamalaan to the Java Island did not survive, the Eastern Harbour District does boast, as might be expected, a number of interesting steel bridges. Although higher-maintenance than concrete, steel constructions were prescribed by the DRO in order to give added emphasis to the unusual character of the bridges. The docks of the islands and the buildings along them, after all, are mostly concrete and brick.

Perhaps due to the influence of the Spanish architect and engineer Santiago Calatrava, who proved, with his bridge in Seville, that bridges can be important landmarks, a lot of attention is being devoted these days to the design of crossings. West 8 designed the two most striking bridges, linking Borneo and Sporenburg. The pedestrian bridge is particularly spectacular: it rises so high above the water that pedestrians have a view over the surrounding residential buildings. This unusual construction allows small pleasure craft to sail under the bridge – this is not the case for the other, flat bridge located further to the west, intended for less physically able pedestrians and cyclists.

The sides of the bridges are made out of three girders linked and twisted together; these girders are composed of red-painted T-shaped beams. A construction of multiple girders is not a new principle, but it has seldom been applied in such an expressive way. However exceptional their design, these bridges will not become true landmarks: they are situated somewhat out of the way, just a little too far off the beaten path. The status of landmark is in the cards, however, for the Jan Schaefer Bridge, which shoots right through the Willem de Zwijger warehouse and spans the IJhaven, linking the Oostelijke Handelskade with the Java Island.

This bridge was designed by Ton Venhoeven C.S. Like in West 8's bridge, the bridge structure has an organic shape.

The architect calls it a lizard slowly crawling across the water. The bridge derives its dynamic character in large part from the different lanes, each crossing the IJhaven in its own rhythm – the car lanes have been kept much more flat than the pedestrian lanes. The expertly finished construction elements reinforce its dynamic character. Most bridges derive their character from their construction; they are little more than its stylized form. Venhoeven explicitly wanted to give the Jan Schaefer Bridge a less image-defining construction. The experience of crossing was not to be dominated by over-intrusive supporting elements. This meant keeping the construction height to a minimum. This was achieved by using an amazing mix of principles. Gerber, Vierendeel and Volle Wand girders are incorporated in the bridge, and everything rests on slender V-shaped columns. The bridge is at its most beautiful above the docks – the carriage deck is at its most slender and elegant there. For the bridge sections, sandwich panels have been used, comparable to a wing profile, except that they are 20 metres long. In the middle the panels are 600 millimetres thick, but toward the sides they taper off to a mere 200 mm. Another striking feature is that two of the bridge sections are fully removable. This was necessary in order to allow the so-called Tall Ships that visit the city during Sail events to pass through.

Elevation
The fact that the freedom of designers increases as span and load decrease is evidenced by the nine different little bridges that cross the four artificial little canals of the Java Island. In order to underscore the rather odd presence of canals in this rough environment, the Amsterdam Art Foundation held a design competition, won by Belgian artists Monica Droste and Guy Rombouts. The bridges were given names like 'idee' ('idea'), 'image', 'conscience', 'enseignement' ('teaching') and 'society' – names that were to be primarily evoked by the rail-ings. The railings are more than simply a design component: they are an extension of the transverse ribs that are welded to the copper structure under the bridge deck.

With these canals, architect Sjoerd Soeters segmented the Java Island. This was his solution for avoiding very long – and possibly somewhat dull – docks. The canals are 1.5 metres deep. This might seem a rather random choice, but a bicycle thrown into the water sinks out of sight. This, in any event, makes these canals very much like those in the city centre.

Soeters' urban-planning concept caused a certain number of civil-engineering problems. The original docks had to be excavated, and they proved to be of massive dimensions. Like on the other islands, the docks on the Java Island are made of thick concrete slabs 15 metres wide, resting on pylons – extra sturdy, because they had to be able to sustain an impact from an ocean-going steamship running adrift.

Making the canals was not just a matter of removing the concrete. Naturally, the island could not be allowed to flood because of the work. The surrounding water was kept away from the islands with special concrete tanks secured to the outer side of the dock walls. Plastic seals filled with alpine grass made this waterproof. This grass is as sturdy as it is flexible and could accommodate any irregularity in the dock wall. After the canals were excavated, definitive concrete tanks were built and the provisional facilities could be removed.

The area between the docks is for the most part filled with sand. This construction, dating back more than a century, was of such quality that the islands could be put to new use with relatively few major interventions. In some places the dock walls had to be reinforced and some of the soil between the dock walls had to be removed because of pollution. Excavating this soil was less problematic than would normally be the case, because the planned parking garages had to be built underground anyway. In the end they did not vanish underground entirely. Their roofs, which can be walked on, are 1.5 metres above the dock surface. The advantage of this is they are now situated just above the groundwater level. This made construction a lot cheaper. In addition, this elevation makes the surrounding water visible from the middle of the island as well. This remarkable effect was hit upon during an exploratory stroll around Borneo by the designers involved in the project. From the middle of the island, only the next island was visible. No trace of the water could be seen. However, from the tops of mounds of coal that had been left behind, the water could indeed be seen, and the special character of the place was immediately palpable. In order to achieve this effect on all the islands, they were made to 'bulge', just enough, in the middle.

Tough contours

The new housing construction on the islands begins right where the original concrete docks end. This avoided the need for expensive building work. Only in two places were the original pier dimensions altered. Aside from Soeters' canals on the Java Island, urban planner Jo Coenen had the head of the KNSM Island rounded off. This proved to be another extremely difficult challenge, because the concrete slab at this particular spot was even sturdier and heavier. This was of course a logical place for extra protection, since the risk of a ship striking the dock was highest here. The slab is no less than one metre thick. To keep costs down, the head of the island was not fully rounded off, but now terminates in the shape of a quarter circle.

The remarkable thing is that Coenen's and Soeters' alterations to the contours, for all the effort they cost, do nothing to strengthen the area. Whereas the Jan Schaefer Bridge piercing through the Willem de Zwijger warehouse has something epic about it, both the rounding off of the KNSM Island and and the segmenting of the Java Island with little canals are too subtle an intervention in this rough environment. From its beginnings, this area derived its power from the logic of engineering; there had been no urge to design. A century ago, the infrastructure of the area was set up in order to ship goods in and out efficiently. There was no higher goal. And these original characteristics were precisely the basic principle for the transformation of these abandoned harbours into a high-density residential area. Again: these contour alterations have no place here.

The fact that the atmosphere of the port is still palpable has to do, on the one hand, with the materials in the streets and roadways. The designers have used original materials as much as possible – steel-reinforced concrete slabs on the KNSM Island and the Veemkade, and natural paving stones on the south dock of the Java Island. In addition, the water – and with it the echo of the port – has been kept visible from almost every spot. On the other hand, the preservation of atmosphere has to do with the logic of the new infrastructure layout. Today, like in the past, it is all being done without a lot of fuss, and every intervention can be explained in light of transport flows or noise-abatement requirements. The apparent simplicity and sequence of logical solutions mean that the new infrastructure merges in an entirely natural way with the old, pragmatically set up infrastructure of the harbours. It is as if it had always been this way.

Rietlanden

Water tower on the corner of the Connecting Dam and the Oostelijke Handelskade, around 1910

den, 1980s

Rietlanden, 1980s

ietlanden under construction, 1999

Rietlanden under construction, 1999

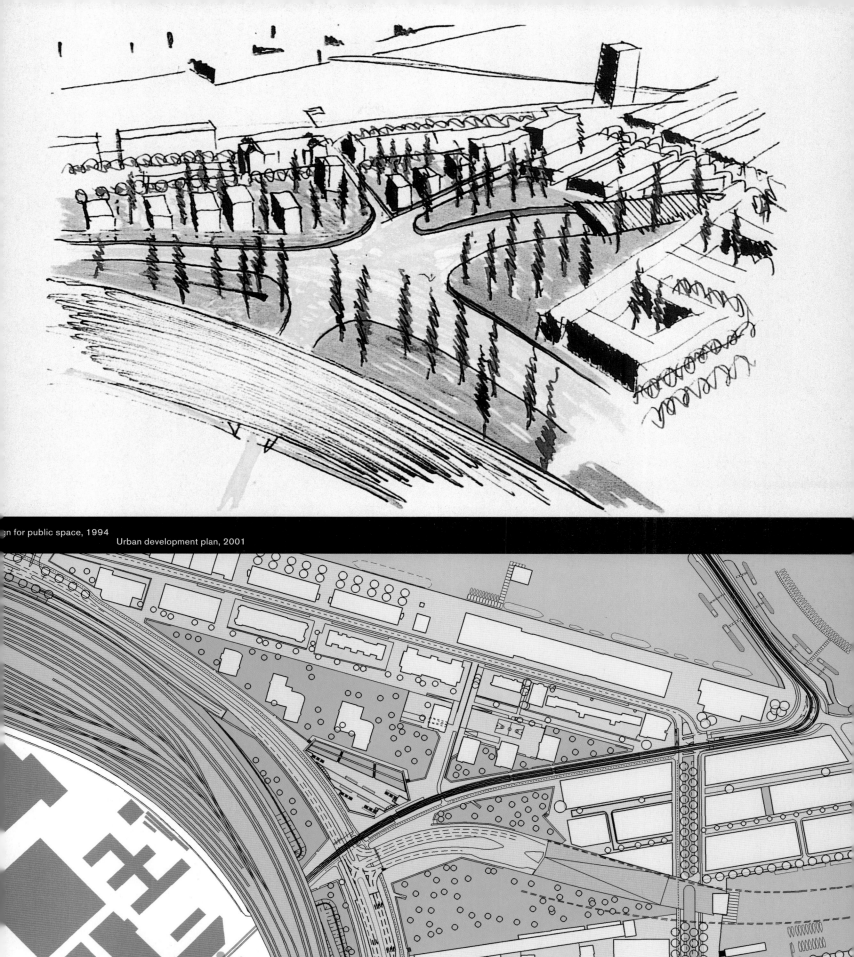

Urban development plan, 2001

Piet Heinkade with route for the IJtram and railroad track

Rietlanden
Marlies Buurman

The layout of the central area dubbed the Rietlanden is the final piece of the Eastern Harbour District. Once the trans-shipment area of the harbour, it must now accommodate all the main access ways for the surrounding peninsulas, making the Rietlanden the pivot point, not only in a spatial sense but also from a traffic-engineering standpoint, between the Eastern Harbour District and the city centre. In addition, the entrance to the Piet Hein Tunnel is located in the middle of this area, which has made the Rietlanden an important access gateway to the city for several years.

The urban plan for the Rietlanden, due to its complex infrastructure, was devised by the Spatial Planning Department (Dienst Ruimtelijke Ordening, or DRO) (Hans Heskamp). The firm of Sant & Co was brought in for the design of the public space. Not only was the infrastructure a complicating

factor, so was the city's aim to build 1,000 dwellings here in addition to office buildings and shopping and community facilities. Because legislation on noise nuisance forbids the construction of housing near busy roadways, a decision was made early in the design process to construct a large open space between the roadways and the buildings. This open area was designed as a park (the Rietlandpark) with a lot of greenery, as well as playground and sports facilities. On the north side, nine silver-coloured residential and office towers by Venhoeven C.S. and Hans van Heeswijk were positioned as free-standing building volumes in the greenery. At the foot of the towers lies a transfer stop between the express tram to IJburg and tram line 10, which has been extended from the Czaar Peterbuurt area to the Azartplein on the KNSM-laan. The stop has been built below the surface level and, for public-safety considerations, in sight of the surrounding roadways and offices. The entrance to the stop is characterized by a wide embankment on the north side, which incorporates

Access to the Piet Heintunnel from the Panamalaan

View of the offices and the residential towers in the Rietlandpark

amalaan

orneokade

stairwells. This incline is clad in granite blocks over which a thin layer
water flows.
Besides the tram line, a three-pronged set of automobile carriageways
sects the Rietlanden. In order to create cohesion for this segmented area,
e expanses of green in between have been raised. In a design by Sant & Co,
ese plateaus were planted with more than 200 Italian poplar trees, and
e grass was seeded with different species of flowers that give the park
different colour in each season. The edges of the raised grass pitches
ere finished with redoubts, walls of steel braiding filled with fragments of
atural stone.
The Rietlandpark is to be surrounded by several areas, each with its
wn character and structure. The urban plan makes no attempt to link these
gether or attenuate the boundaries between them. The building structure
Borneo and Sporenburg even continues into the Rietlandpark

the time of the Royal Netherlands Steamship Company (KNSM). These buildings have or will be given new functions. The former hydraulic power station
by B. de Greef and W. Springer (1885), for example, was converted into the
restaurant-nightclub Panama, and the Lloyd Hotel by architect E. Breman
(1918) has been renovated and converted, in a design by MVRDV, into a hotel
for artists and art lovers.
    On the opposite side of the roadway will come Nieuw Argentinië, an
elongated building that connects with the buildings on the Oostelijke Handelskade. West of this stands a row of buildings constructed earlier, including two
residential buildings by Frits van Dongen (1995) and a covered shopping
centre designed by Willem Jan Neutelings. By using the iron framework and
the trussed roof of the former coffee and cocoa hangar Brazilië, Neutelings
created an open building with lateral passageways that link the Oostelijke
Handelskade with the IJ-haven. Below ground there is a parking garage

Rietlandterras with the residential building Hoop, Liefde en Fortuin

and the Verbindingsdam (Connecting Dam), was also designed by Neutelings and houses a supermarket and a parking level in addition to 67 apartments. The white tower is visible from afar and marks the transition between the various sections of the area.

The southern boundary of the Rietlandpark is indicated by a monumental, angled residential building by Rudy Uytenhaak. The building houses more than 300 flats in the rental as well as the owner-occupied sector. The complex consists of surfaces that cross and overlap one another, clad in different materials. The inclined north façade consists of a concrete screen in which the windows are deeply recessed. The front serves as a 'veil': only when one gets closer do the black dots on the concrete (a pattern by artist Willem Oorebeek) and the flats behind it become visible.

The public space has a large role to play in the Rietlanden. The character of the area is in large part defined by the green park, which like the water in the surrounding

is also characterized by other sites with a special layout. The northern Veemkade, on the IJhaven, for example, has been made into a boulevard with restricted automobile access, with a yacht marina and a floating cinema behind the shopping centre. The dock is paved with steel-reinforced concrete slabs, reminiscent of the harbour. To demarcate the division between the cyclist and pedestrian traffic, a line of stainless-steel studs has been laid down in the heart of the strip of concrete slabs. Another remarkable spot is the roof of the Piet Hein Tunnel. Here an inclined playground for youngsters has been built, which also accommodates public events. The plaza, clad in scoria bricks, stands out from its surroundings in material and colour. From its highest point (six metres above the Amsterdam ordnance level) it offers a wide view over the Rietlanden.

In the middle of the Rietlanden, near the tram transfer stop, stands a work of art by Frank Mandersloot. It is made up of a stack of four huge

rientations of the surrounding buildings. The tables are a reference to
text by Lawrence Weiner (from *Notities over een tafel* ('Notes concerning
table'), 1988): 'This city. This Amsterdam built on pylons sunk into the
nud and the mire. This city built on pylons standing on the stand is therefore
table. A table for the presentation of work.'

82 architecture firm **UN Studio** project architect **Ben van Berkel, Harrie Pappot** project **Piet Hein Tunnel** programme **entrance and ventilation building** client **Combinatie PHT,**
msterdam design/completion **1990/1996**

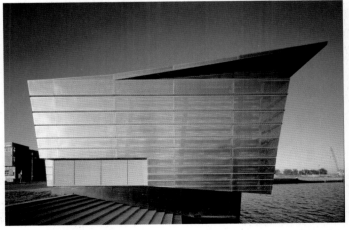

179 architecture firm **Architectenbureau K. van Velsen**   project architect **Koen van Velsen**   project **Nieuw Argentinië**   programme **121 lofts, 60 apartments (private sector) and 80 rental dwellings (public sector)**   client **Het Oosten housing corporation, Amsterdam**   design/completion **1998/2006**

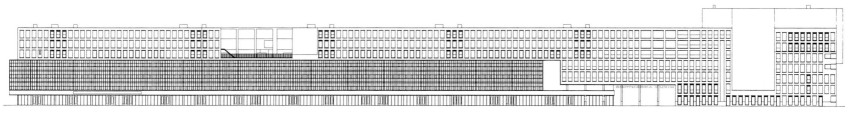

north façade

south façade

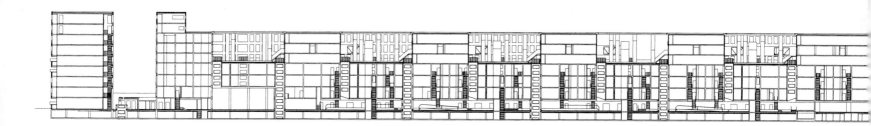

181/182 architecture firm **de Architecten Cie.**   project architect **Frits van Dongen**   project **My Side**   programme **108 rental dwellings (private sector)**   client **Amstelland Vastgoed, Amsterdam**   design/completion **1991/1995**

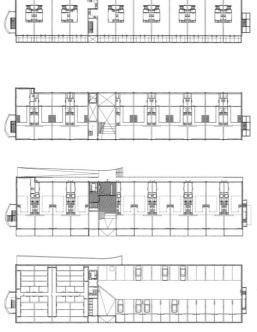

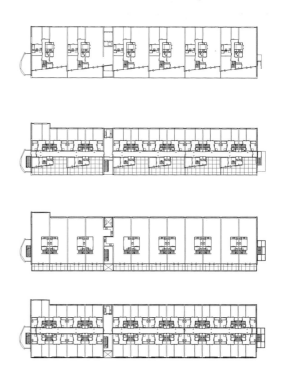

The Lloyd Hotel by architect E. Breman, 1918

198 architecture firm **Hans van Heeswijk architecten**   project architect **Hans van Heeswijk**   project **Cineship cinema**   programme **new façade design**   client **Cinemien, Amsterdam**
design/completion **2000/2004**

194 architecture firm **Hans van Heeswijk architecten** project architect **Hans van Heeswijk** project **Quintet Office Park** programme **5 office towers, parking garage** client **Amplan Vastgoed, Amsterdam** design/completion **1998/2001**

195 architecture firm **Claus en Kaan Architecten** project architect **Kees Kaan** project **Rietlanden** programme **35 rental dwellings, 54 owner-occupied dwellings, 6 commercial spaces**
client **De Principaal, Amsterdam** design/completion **1996/2000**

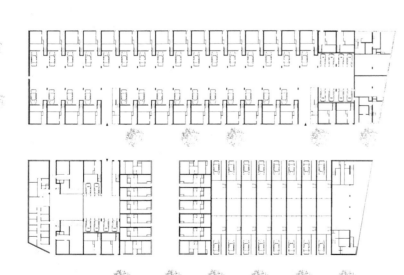

ground floor

199 architecture firm **Hans van Heeswijk architecten** project architect **Hans van Heeswijk** project **bridges and stops for the IJtram** programme **design of all civil artworks, such as moving and permanent bridges, viaducts, tunnels and platform constructions for the IJtram** client **City IJtram Project Bureau, Amsterdam** design/completion **1998/2004**

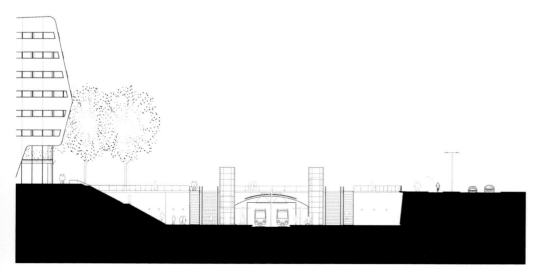

184/185 architecture firm **Neutelings Riedijk Architecten** project architect **Willem Jan Neutelings, Michiel Riedijk** project **Brazilië shopping centre and residential tower** programme **shopping centre with underground parking garage, 68 dwellings (private sector) with parking deck** client **Blauwhoed, Rotterdam and Eurowoningen, Rotterdam** design/completion **1993/1998**

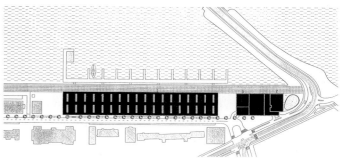

architecture firm **Rudy Uytenhaak architectenbureau**   project architect **Rudy Uytenhaak, Engbert van der Zaag**   project **Hoop, Liefde en Fortuin**

programme **167 owner-occupied dwellings, 202 public-sector rental dwellings, parking garage (223 spaces), welfare centre/day-care centre**   client **Woningbedrijf Amsterdam and Bouwfonds Wonen**   design/completion **1996/2002**

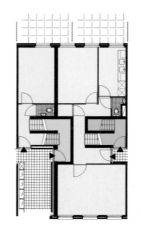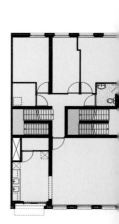

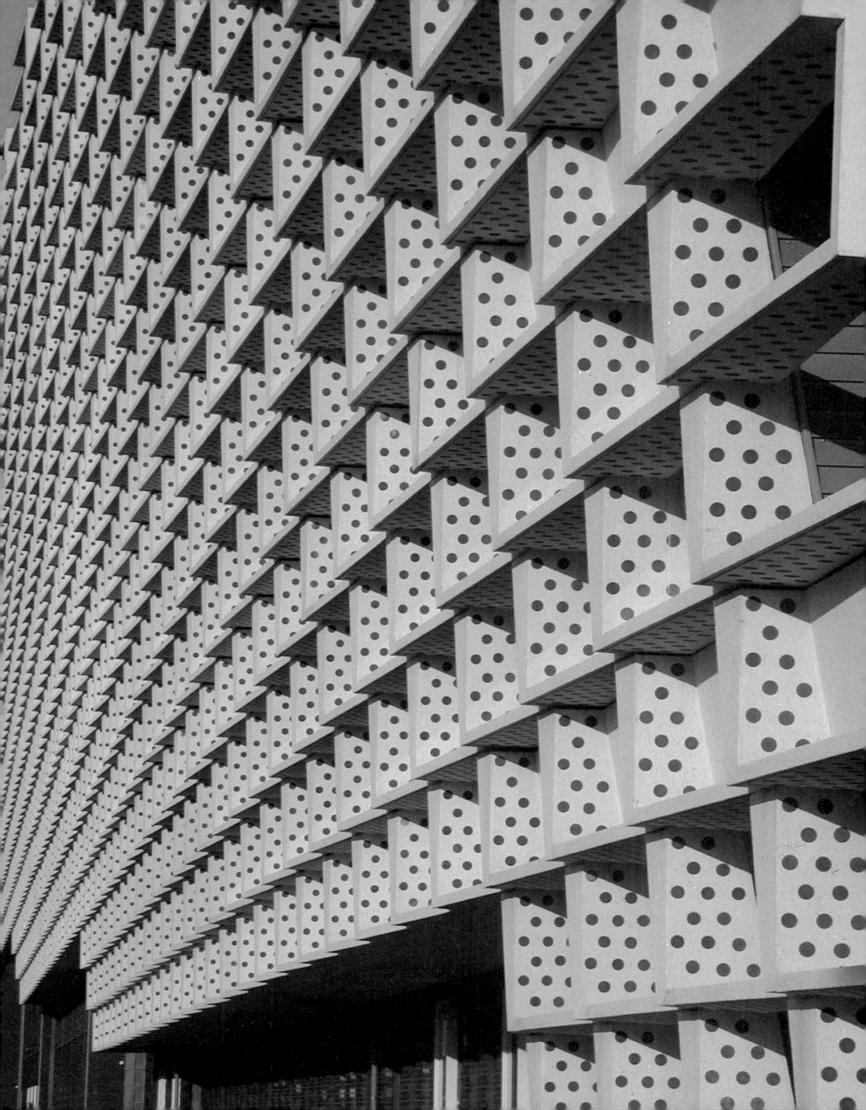

193 architecture firm **Venhoeven C.S.** project architect **Ton Venhoeven** project **Park towers De Rietlanden** programme **120 private-sector dwellings, 36 public-sector rental dwellings, commercial spaces, 3 parking garages (147 spaces)** client **Zomers Buiten housing corporation, Amsterdam (dwellings), City Real Estate Department, Amsterdam (parking garages)** design/completion **1995/2001**

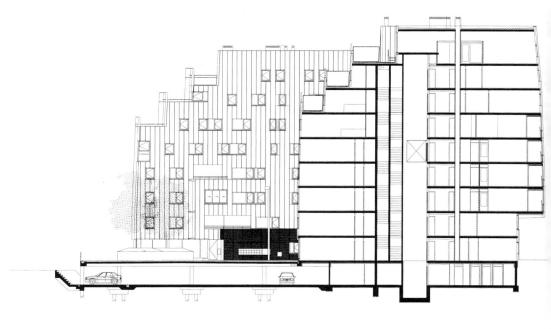

1 architecture firm **de Architecten Cie.**   project architect **Frits van Dongen**   project **Batavia**   programme **167 apartments, 1100 m² of office space, parking space (136 spaces)**
ent **De Principaal, Amsterdam**   design/completion **1997/2000**

11

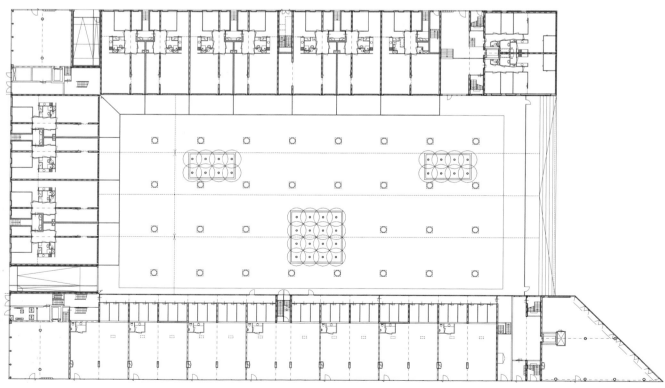

ground floor

Eastern islands
Super-Vinex suburb in Amsterdam

Bernard Hulsman

The Java Island enrages some people. When I was paying a visit to the artist Pjotr Müller in 1998, he practically began foaming at the mouth when the Java Island came up. From his studio on the De Ruyterkade near the Central Station in Amsterdam, this maker of architectural sculptures had a distant view of this peninsula. Müller thought it 'criminal' that four small canals have been dug on the Java Island. At the end of the twentieth century it was absurd, he said, to imitate Amsterdam's seventeenth-century ring of inner canals. This was fraud – no, worse, the Java Island was a reactionary lie. There was only one thing for it, he said: the Java Island must be bombed. Not that he thought such a proposition was very likely to be carried out.

Müller had good things to say, on the other hand, about another new residential development he could see from his window: the IJplein, right on the other side of the IJ. This former shipyard in Amsterdam-Noord was developed in the early 1980s according to an urban design by the Office for Metropolitan Architecture, Rem Koolhaas' firm. My noting that Koolhaas had also borrowed from urban-planning history for the IJplein and that his design looked a lot like a German Neu Bau residential district from the 1920s failed to impress Müller. No, Koolhaas' IJplein was 'modern', 'current' and therefore 'good', he thought. It was a scandal that Amsterdam had commissioned something as retarded as the Java Island.

Müller was expressing a viewpoint widely shared among artists with an interest in architecture, as well as among architects and critics, in the 1990s. Koolhaas' neo-modernist urbanism could bank on the admiration of many, especially young architects. His scenario method – Koolhaas had projected all

manner of well-known modernist urban designs onto the IJplein and out of this distilled a new design – would be followed many times, primarily by young architects. Koolhaas' neo-modernism became the Dutch architecture style par excellence during the first half of the 1990s. However, the City of Amsterdam's Spatial Planning Department (Dienst Ruimtelijke Ordening, or DRO) had decided as early as the second half of the 1980s that the IJplein definitely deserved no follow-up. Upon completion of the IJplein, the department was less than satisfied with the layout of the neighbourhood. For the KSNM Island, the first of four eastern, disused peninsulas the city of Amsterdam wanted to fill with residential units, in any event, the DRO wanted no repeat of the IJplein, with its 100 percent public-sector, low-density housing and its strip construction perpendicular to the IJ, which meant most residents had very little in the way of a view on the water. The KNSM Island had to be a distinct urbanist ensemble with a distinct relation to the abundant water surrounding the peninsula.

So it was no surprise that Jo Coenen was selected in 1989 to elaborate the DRO's structural sketches for the KNSM Island. Jo Coenen had shown in earlier designs that he was one of the few Dutch architects who were not afraid of the monumental. He had given the renovated Vaillantlaan, a long street through an urban regeneration area in The Hague, a monumental grandeur, with long façades constructed from a limited number of elements.

With the urban design that Jo Coenen created within the framework set up by the DRO, Amsterdam did indeed get a sort of elongated variant of Berlage's Amsterdam Plan-Zuid (South Plan) on the KNSM Island. In fact, Coenen's design is more evocative of nineteenth-century monumental urbanism than Plan-Zuid itself. A broad boulevard in the middle of the narrow island is flanked on one side by closed and on the other by semi-open residential blocks and dead-ends somewhat disappointingly at a round apartment complex designed by Coenen himself. The gigantic residential blocks on the south side of the KSNM Island, in particular, are more monumental than anything found in Berlage's completed Plan-Zuid.

Of these mighty constructions, Kollhoff and Rapp's dark, sculptural colossus would incidentally become one of the most influential buildings in 1990s Dutch architecture.

When the KNSM Island was completed halfway through the 1990s, the choice of Coenen's monumental urban architecture turned out to be a break with Amsterdam's urban development tradition. From the Second World War onwards, the modernist tradition had always been a strong factor in the city's urban planning. Until the mid-1970s, in fact, modernism had held the monopoly. During the first decades following the war, it was hard-core modernist Cornelis van Eesteren, as head of the Town Planning department, who defined Amsterdam's urban planning. Not only were open residential blocks and building strips the determining elements in the Westelijke Tuinsteden garden suburbs, but Van Eesteren and his department applied the principles of modernist urbanism in Buitenveldert as well, and even in the section of Amsterdam-Zuid that actually fell under Berlage's Plan-Zuid but was not yet completed in 1945.

The apotheosis of Amsterdam's modernist urbanism came with the Bijlmermeer, a new city district for 100,000 inhabitants that, entirely in keeping with Le Corbusier's principles of separation of functions and traffic types, became a city of high-rise buildings amidst abundant greenery. Outside the circles of architects and architecture initiates, this district is generally considered one of the greatest urban-planning failures in the Netherlands of the twentieth century. However, because many architects, including Kees Rijnboutt, one of the designers of the gallery-flat buildings in the Bijlmer, to this day view the Bijlmermeer as a successful residential estate, most of it now being torn down entirely without justification, the Bijlmermeer debacle did not spell the end of modernism in Amsterdam's urban planning. Carel Weeber's rationalist design for the Venserpolder, in the early 1980s, may have brought the closed residential block with entrance halls back into the city's urban architecture, but this was countered with the fact that Koolhaas' above-mentioned design for the IJplein, with its strip construction and open surfaces as public space, was undiluted modernism. On the Abattoir (Slaughterhouse) site and the

Entrepotdok, redeveloped several years after the IJplein, Koolhaas' old-fashioned strip construction was not as rigorously applied, but most of the residential blocks are nevertheless semi-open. In retrospect, it was here, in the first section of the Eastern Harbour islands to be packed with dwellings, that the first, hesitant steps were taken toward the closed residential blocks of the KNSM Island.

With the KNSM Island, Amsterdam bid farewell to modernist urbanism – one of the first Dutch cities to do so. On the three peninsulas that were developed after the KNSM Island – the Java Island and the twin islands Borneo and Sporenburg – strip construction would not be coming back either. The same applies for IJburg, the Amsterdam Vinex suburb currently under construction: the closed residential block will predominate here also. The Eastern Harbour islands are a departure from Amsterdam's urban development from a social point of view as well. Whereas until the end of the 1980s new residential developments in Amsterdam consisted for the most part of public-sector rental units, on the Java Island, Borneo-Sporenburg and, to a somewhat lesser extent, the KNSM Island, owner-occupied dwellings predominate.

On the Java Island and Borneo-Sporenburg, respectively, Sjoerd Soeters and Adriaan Geuze, of the landscape architecture firm West 8, have borrowed from old examples of urbanism. As Pjotr Müller quite rightly saw, Sjoerd Soeters took inspiration for his design for the Java Island from Amsterdam's famous seventeenth-century ring of inner canals. And Adriaan Geuze, responsible for the urban design of Borneo and Sporenburg, has more than once compared his designs for these islands with the Jordaan, the now beloved, densely built Amsterdam neighbourhood built on a meadow outside the ring of inner canals in the seventeenth century. Yet, just as the KNSM Island is no repeat of Plan-Zuid – how could it be? – the Java Island and Borneo-Sporenburg are no slavish imitations of the old city quarters. Along the long north and south docks of the Java Island, for instance, Soeters placed not individual canal houses, as is the case along the old historic canals, but massive apartment buildings of seven to ten and then five to seven levels. Soeters prescribed six types of buildings for the docks, each 27 metres wide and each with dwellings intended for different target groups with presumably different lifestyles. The long façades were intersected by four small, narrow canals, along which individual houses were in fact built. They consist of a total of 56 very narrow canal houses, designed by 19 young architects and placed along the canals in a different order each time. This was a way to break the monotony that threatened to dominate the new Java Island, and it resulted in four quasi-closed blocks and one semi-open block on the island, with the apartment complexes on the long sides and the canal houses on the short sides.

In another departure from the often deep gardens behind the houses along Amsterdam's historic canals, the car-free court-yards of the residential blocks on the Java Island are not private property, but small public parks with hillocks here and there, as well as sculptures, designed by artists, as points of interest. In these pleasantly shut-away courtyards, the garden sheds one might find in the old canal gardens have grown, as it were, into blocks of flats. Soeters has also worked the level variations found in the old Amsterdam canals into the Java Island. The four little canals are a metre and a half lower than the north and south docks, and the bridges over the canals are bow-shaped, so that they, just like the bridges in the old part of Amsterdam, create a gently rolling streetscape.

Of the three urban designs devised for the four Eastern Harbour islands, Adriaan Geuze's design for Borneo and Sporenburg is the furthest removed from a historic model. In his initial design for Borneo-Sporenburg Geuze proposed filling the two parallel islands with 'high-density low-rise buildings'. For these low-rise buildings, Geuze took inspiration from villages in the former Zuiderzee, where little houses along the dikes braved the watery expanses of the former inland sea. Geuze felt the low-rise buildings should consist of long, narrow houses with their backs to one another. They would be situated according to a strict allotment of built and open strips that would consistently run perpendicular to the direction of the docks. Because of this, Geuze's original design can be interpreted as

a curious variation on modernist strip construction. Since such a construction would not deliver the DRO's target density of 100 housing units per hectare, Geuze also included three so-called 'meteorites' in the plan, 'superblocks' of flats.

Although Geuze's urban design for Borneo-Sporenburg was selected, the commissioners of the project development company specially set up for these islands, New Deal, were not convinced of the plan's feasibility. After further research, the plans for the 'sea of houses' were modified. The low-rise build-ings in strips were replaced by enclosed blocks of contiguous residential units with light-yards, roof terraces and ground-floor access. The houses would still be set back to back, so that gardens would remain unknown on Borneo-Sporenburg. The broad outlines of Geuze's urban plan – the combination of high-density low-rise buildings with three superblocks – were not significantly affected, but there were major consequences for the eventual streetscape. An urban design grounded in modernist tenets mutated into a traditionalist design: instead of 'supermodernist' streets of low-rises in strips, streets with closed façades were built.

To elaborate plans for the low-rise dwellings and the three meteorites, a selection of architects were brought in, who had to observe urban-planning stipulations regarding building height and material use. A flat roof was also mandated for every house. A small portion of Borneo was allotted in 60 free-hold parcels. Yet there was no question of any real freedom here, either, and the architects chosen by the parcel owners had to adhere to guidelines for building height, alignments and building width. Through his strict construction requirements, Geuze was explicitly seeking unity and uniformity, rather than variety.

A visit to the Eastern Harbour District involuntarily conjures up the thought that this was actually what was intended with the Vinex districts, the new suburban residential developments currently under construction everywhere. Compact new residential developments near or in the larger cities of the Netherlands – that was what Dutch suburbs were supposed to become around the turn of the millennium, according to the

Dutch government's Addendum to the Fourth National Policy Document on Spatial Planning (Vierde Nota Ruimtelijke Ordening Extra, or Vinex) in 1991. And this is exactly what the KNSM Island, the Java Island and Borneo-Sporenburg have become. The similarities between the average Vinex district, as it is currently being built in the Netherlands, and the eastern harbour islands are manifold. Just like the new Dutch suburbs, the new eastern islands are first and foremost residential developments. And just as many Vinex districts have a small business park that serves as a buffer between a motorway and the houses, the office buildings of the eastern islands are situated near the busy traffic hub, where the access way to the Java Island and the KNSM Island and the motorway through the new Piet Hein Tunnel begin. Not far away there is a shopping centre, where all island residents can go for their everyday purchases – in this the Eastern Harbour District is no different from a suburb either. Furthermore, the eastern islands have in common with most Vinex districts that a small portion of the area is reserved for free-hold parcels. And just as most new suburbs, despite all the fine promises, still have no good public-transport connections to the cities to which they are attached, it is only in the near future, about seven years after the completion of the KNSM Island, that a new tramline to the new eastern islands will go into operation. The islands, like most new Dutch suburbs, are also located close to an express-way. Island residents need only drive their cars through the Piet Hein Tunnel, under the water between Borneo and Sporen-burg, to reach Amsterdam's ring motorway.

In two areas, however, the new eastern islands surpass the average Dutch Vinex district with ease. The building density of the islands, at about 100 housing units per hectare, is almost three times as high, which makes them nearly as densely built as the Concertgebouw quarter, for instance, a beloved, densely built, traditional metropolitan area in Amsterdam-Zuid. The islands are also located much closer to the old city centre than the average Vinex district. A bicycle ride from the historic canal area to the KNSM Island or Borneo-Sporenburg takes no more than about 20 minutes. The Java Island can be reached even faster, thanks to the construction of the Jan Schaefer Bridge, designed by Ton Venhoeven C.S., and a new ferry service between the western tip of the island and the Central Station.

The compact Vinex districts raised expectations that, unlike in the older suburbs, an 'urbanity' would emerge there, something the older suburbs sorely missed. Now that a several Vinex districts have been completed, it must be concluded that this expectation has not been met. Most Vinex districts have ended up as familiar residential developments dominated by row-houses, where urban functions like housing, employment, shopping and recreation are not mixed, but instead are rele-gated each to its own separate location. The main reason for this lack of urbanity is often attributed to the fact that the Vinex districts, in the end, were designed with a much lower building density than was originally intended. This supposedly generates too little support for such traditional urban amenities as a corner café. Vinex districts are often depicted as neither fish nor flesh, not metropolitan but not really suburban either.

Yet the eastern islands demonstrate that even a tripling of the Vinex density does not lead to urbanity as we know it in old city centres. For, on the eastern islands, there is hardly any urbanity to be found, except for a section of the KNSM Island. Here, in Loods 6, a renovated former dock hangar, businesses and shops have been set up. Shops, businesses and a café have also opened in the ground levels of Kollhoff's Piraeus building and Bruno Albert's block. But that is not enough to create a lively environment like that of the old city centre, or of an Amsterdam neighbourhood with a comparable housing density, like the Concertgebouw quarter. The Java Island and Borneo-Sporenburg show an even greater lack of urbanity: on these islands one can find no more than the odd stray restaurant.

And so the eastern islands, despite their dense construction, have acquired a suburban character. The suburbanity is especially apparent on Borneo-Sporenburg. For, while the KNSM Island and the Java Island are packed with metropolitan apartment buildings, suburban low-rises predominate on

Borneo-Sporenburg. Geuze may like to compare his islands with the Jordaan, but Borneo-Sporenburg lacks not only the hustle and bustle, shops, cafés and restaurants, but also the varied architecture of that part of town. And for all that the long buildings with light-yards evoke the old building with entrance halls and front and back flats in old Amsterdam, the succession of low-rise buildings on Borneo-Sporenburg, all the same height and invariably finished in dark brick, mostly look like familiar row-houses.

Contemporary urban planning is apparently organized in such a way that an intricate mixture of functions, such as that found in older Amsterdam neighbourhoods, can no longer be created even in the densely built new sections of the city. The deregulation of housing construction implemented in the early 1990s plays a definite part in this. The housing corporations were privatized and the housing construction subsidies abolished. Housing construction and urban planning became primarily commercial enterprises, within which the 'demands of the market' had to be taken into account. And these demands were interpreted by builders in such a way that there was no room for many spaces for shops and eating and drinking establishments and other amenities that made older neighbourhoods so attractive. At most, project developers build houses that are so large that the resident can set up an office at home, but when it comes to shops and the like, they favour shopping centres with many spaces for big secure tenants like Albert Heijn and Etos, instead of little corner shops for dodgy tenants like small grocers and other fast-disappearing shopkeepers.

The view the builders of the Eastern Harbour islands have of the demands of the market is probably accurate. The islands, after all, are located so close to the old city, with its wealth of amenities, that island residents can easily make use of those as well. Moreover, it is clear that grocers and other small shopkeepers find it no easier to keep their heads above water, if at all, in the Amsterdam city centre. This makes the building of spaces for small-scale urban facilities a risky proposition. In addition, there is little reason to believe that the residents of Amsterdam's islands behave much differently from the suburban residents who evolved during the 1990s into network-city dwellers. The Vinex districts were built to reinforce the 'compact city', but they increasingly turn out to be part of a network city. The old city centres are not the hubs of this network city; rather they are simply junctions in a network, along with many other destinations. The Vinex resident is no longer the traditional suburbanite oriented for work, shopping and recreation toward the centre of the city to which the suburb is attached. The mobile network-city dweller does not need to live in a neighbourhood with a lot of amenities – he seeks and finds these in his surroundings himself. Today's suburbanite views his Vinex house as a base, from which he, by car of course, puts together his own city from among a large number of destinations within a wide radius. He lives in a Vinex district, works in an industrial estate along the motorway 30 kilometres away, goes out to eat in a restaurant along another motorway, practices a sport in a sports facility in the middle of a meadow, goes to the movies in a megaplex in another suburb, shops in the Batavia Stad shopping mall near Lelystad and, yes, once in a while makes a day trip to the old city. The residents of the Eastern Harbour islands probably make more use of the old city than the Vinex district resident, but for the rest they can construct their own network city, from their light-yard dwelling on Borneo-Sporenburg, for instance, just as well as any Vinex resident. The Eastern Harbour islands have become something like super-Vinex districts – super-compact residential developments superclose to the old city centre.

Oostelijke Handelskade

Oostelijke Handelskade, around 1920

telijke Handelskade, 1980s

Oostelijke Handelskade, 1980s

Oostelijke Handelskade, end 1990s

elijke Handelskade around 1910

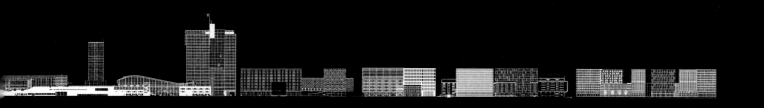

View of the Oostelijke Handelskade from the Javakade

View of the Oostelijke Handelskade from the Bogortuin garden

Oostelijke Handelskade
Marlies Buurman

From the end of the nineteenth century, a long row of warehouses defined the appearance of the two-kilometre-long Oostelijke Handelskade dock on the IJ-haven. Many of these striking buildings lost their function in the 1970s and were demolished; others continued to be used for a long time by squatters and artists.

The Oostelijke Handelskade now forms an important link between the regenerated Eastern Harbour District and the city centre. The importance of this link function was reinforced by the opening of the Piet Hein Tunnel in 1997. With this tunnel, which opens in the middle of the central area of the Eastern Harbour District, Amsterdam got a new city entrance from the ring road. The construction of the IJ tram, which runs via the Oostelijke Handelskade and connects the city centre with the centre of IJburg in 18 minutes, makes the dock an important link.

The development of the Oostelijke Handelskade is formally part of the city's project for the banks of the IJ and is administratively set out in the policy document 'Ankers in het IJ' ('Anchors in the IJ', 1995). This policy document proposes a gradual development for the south bank of the IJ. It consists of a chain of islands and docks on either side of the Central Station, once built to moor ships, shunt trains and load and unload cargo. These areas have long since lost their functions and offer not only marvelous sites for future living and work areas, but also the opportunity to restore the relationship between the city centre and the IJ. For this reason, important sites have been designated to strengthen that relationship. The westernmost section of the Oostelijke Handelskade is one of these 'anchors'.

Commissioned by the South Bank of the IJ Project Group, Hans van der Made of the Spatial Planning Department (Dienst Ruimtelijke Ordening, or DRO) devised an urban plan in 1997 based on an earlier study by the Office for Metropolitan Architecture (OMA). Important sources of inspiration

View of the Oostelijke Handelskade and the IJhaven from the Bogortuin garden

Oostelijke Handelskade with the Java Island in the background

include the long lines of the Veemkade along the water, the railroad dike and the carriageway that runs parallel to it, the Piet Heinkade. The DRO's plan foresees a mixture of old warehouses and new construction along the dock in the coming years. Preserved buildings will get new functions and will be surrounded by dwellings, offices, collective commercial buildings and cultural facilities. This programme is to be housed in a sequence of tall, solid buildings that are meant to give the area a metropolitan character. All the buildings will stand atop a plinth in which parking garages will be located. The difference between the buildings on the dock and those on the carriageway is significant. On the IJ side, the new construction must form a single visual rampart with the warehouses. On the city side, free-standing buildings will be located, and they will be quite a bit taller. Between the rampart and the free-standing buildings will be an open zone 12 metres wide, creating a visual link along the length of the long dock.

For the development of the dock, a partitioning into different planning areas was chosen, each to be elaborated by a market player with a coordinating architect. The coordinating architects are Hans van Heeswijk, Kees Christiaanse (of KCAP), the architect duo Köther & Salman and Christian Rapp. The easternmost area, Nieuw Amerika, is under Rapp's supervision and is partitioned into three separate buildings each designed by a different architect. The relationship between living and work spaces takes centre stage. The designs for Chicago (Rapp & Rapp), and Boston (DKV Architecten), especially, are made spectacular by the combination of new and old. The new construction is literally wrapped around the old warehouses in both cases. Detroit houses mainly spacious luxury dwellings and was designed by the Belgian architect Bob van Reeth. The heart of the building is a great glass atrium that follows the volume of the building and narrows as it rises. The buildings will be completed in 2005.

Between Nieuw Amerika and the Jan Schaefer Bridge will come the De Loodsen ('The Hangars') area. Here, Köther & Salman, Wingender

View of the Veemkade from the Javakade

Hovenier and Herder Van der Neut are building linked towers around different inner plazas. The complex will house dwellings, offices and commercial spaces. Some of these will be offered in the form of a shell, to stimulate home-based businesses.

To the left of De Loodsen the Pakhuizen (Warehouses) plan will be implemented, coordinated by Kees Christiaanse, which foresees various office and housing-work buildings around three preserved warehouses. The designs are by Branimir Medic (Architekten Cie.), Claus en Kaan, Villanova and Kees Christiaanse. The Azië warehouse was converted by Meyer en Van Schooten into the design centre Het Pakhuis ('The Warehouse') in 1999 and has since become an inspiring example of both respectful restoration and succesful re-allocation.

Under the coordination of Hans van Heeswijk, the adjacent area Nieuw Europa will be built. This area marks the transition from the housing-work function on the greater part of the dock to the office and public funtion on

the western tip. On the IJ side will come a long building by Mastenbroek and Van Gameren, the lower level of which will be constructed as a bus terminal and the upper levels as offices. The buildings on the carriageway side will also house offices.

The westernmost section of the Oostelijke Handelskade, the so-called Kop (Head), is situated at a strategic spot between the new and the old city, a short distance from the Central Station. This site is bound on three sides by water and offers, like the head of the Java Island, countless possibilities for creating a spectacular, urban gesture. The visual importance of the place is all the more underscored by the fact that important shipping routes in the IJ merge near the Kop, giving it a potentially important representative function. A separate master plan has been devised for this Kop, in which the site is seen as a new city crossroads, with the new Muziekgebouw/BIMhuis by the Danish architecture firm Nielsen, Nielsen & Nielsen at its furthest point. It will house concert halls, studios, practice rooms, documentation centres and

eating and drinking establishments. The building incorporates a high glass foyer, into which extend the concert halls of the former music centres the IJsbreker and the BIMhuis. The outer wall is made entirely out of double-glazing, affording visitors a gorgeous view onto the IJ all around. The entrance is dominated by a great marquee. In front of the building will come a plaza with steps extending down to the water.

Immediately behind the music centre will come the Dorint Hotel, designed by Claus en Kaan. The plinth will accommodate public functions, such as a lobby, eating and drinking establishments and conference and exhibition rooms. Above this, the hotel manifests itself as a solid, floating volume, perpendicular to the lower buildings. Next to this site, the architecture firm of Hellmuth Obata + Kassabaum (HOK) has already built the Passenger Terminal Amsterdam, with its monumental undulating roof and the Dexia Bank office building with a large parking garage.

The Dijksgracht, south of the Kop and the railroad tracks, forms an

important link in the route from the Central Station to the music centre, and is entirely predicated on housing on the water. Here, in a quiet innner harbour, about 80 floating dwellings and commercial premises will be situated perpendicular to the dock. There is also to be space for urban amenities such as a plaza that provides a view onto the Oosterdok, and a feasibility study has been conducted into the possibility for a swimming pool in this location. No decision on that has yet been reached. The construction of the Oosterdok Swing Bridge has already started. Cyclists and pedestrians will soon have an important connection between the city centre and the Handelskade.

176 architecture firm **DKV architekten** project architect **Dolf Dobbelaar, Herman de Kovel, Paul de Vroom** project **Nieuw Australië** programme **40 apartments in warehouse**, 0 apartments in new construction, commercial space, 168 parking spaces client **Nieuw Amerika development consortium, Amsterdam** design/completion **1998/2004**

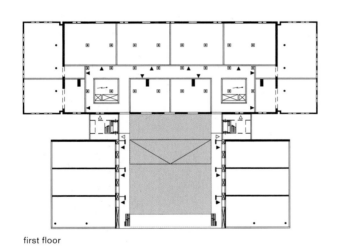

first floor

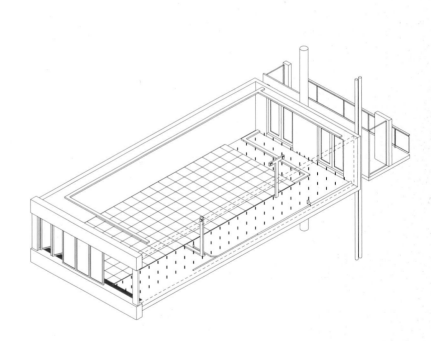

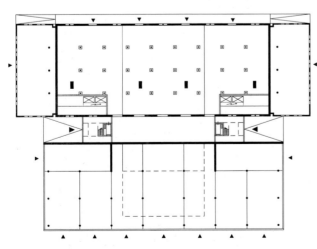

ground floor

169 architecture firm **Meyer en Van Schooten Architecten**   project architect **Roberto Meyer, Jeroen van Schooten**   project **conversion of Pakhuis Amsterdam warehouse**   programme **office, exhibition space for more than 30 different participants/institutions, shipping space, underground parking garage**   client **Pakhuis Amsterdam (formerly Nederlands Interieur Collectief (NIC)), Amsterdam**   design/completion **1996/1999**

73 architecture firm **Villanova architecten**   project architect **Andries Laane, Helene Houben**   project **Pakhuis Afrika warehouse**   programme **offices/businesses, showrooms**
ient **Heijmans IBC Vastgoedontwikkeling, Rosmalen**   design/completion **1998/2005**

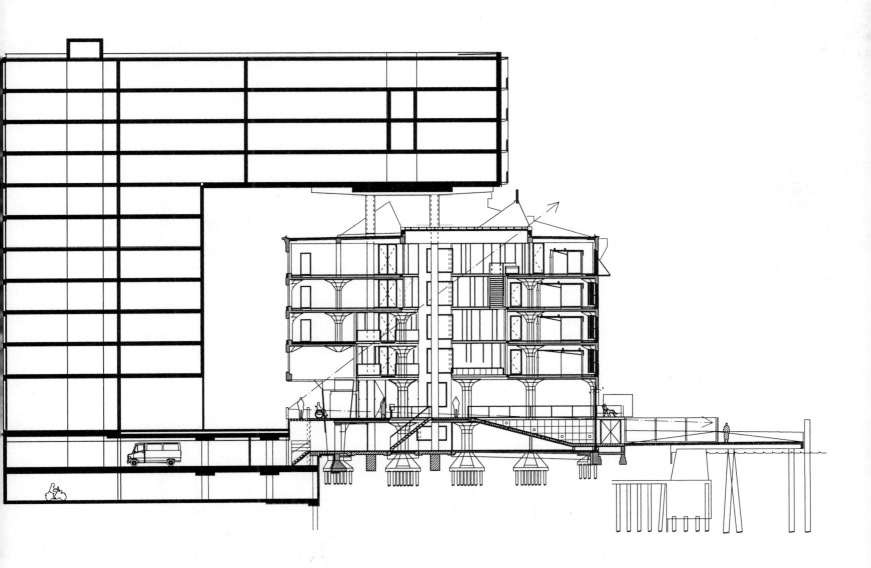

164 architecture firm **Hellmuth Obata + Kassabaum Architects** project architect **Larry Malcic** project **Passenger Terminal Amsterdam** programme **cruiseterminal** client **Amsterdam Port Authority** design/completion **1996/2000**

163 architecture firm **Claus en Kaan Architecten** project architect **Felix Claus** project **Dorint City Harbour** programme **hotel with 364 rooms, convention centre, bus terminal, underground parking garage** client **Amplan Vastgoed, Amsterdam** design/completion **2000/2005**

162 architecture firm **Nielsen, Nielsen & Nielsen**   project architect **Palle Holsting**   project **BIMhuis**   programme **music building**   client **Amsterdam Port Authority**

design/completion **2002/2004**

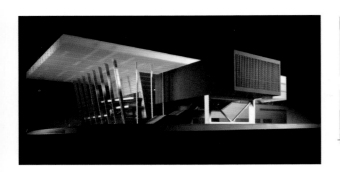

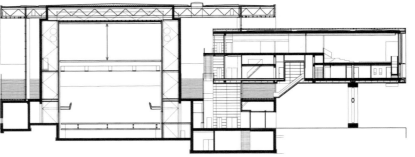

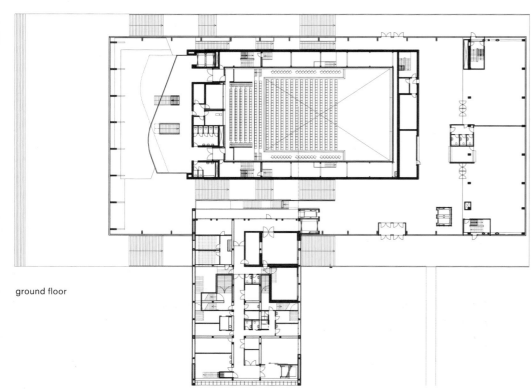

ground floor

168 architecture firm **Hans van Heeswijk architecten**   project architect **Hans van Heeswijk in association with de Architectengroep**   project **Nieuw Europa**   programme **offices, bus terminal, parking garage**   client **Amplan Vastgoed, Amsterdam**   design/completion **2002/2004**

Map of the Eastern Harbour District

The numbers in blue refer to projects included in this publication.

● **Buildings**

Abattoir and Veemarkt sites and Entrepot-West

1 L. Lafour & R. Wijk, 1989
2 F. van Dillen, 1987
3 B. Mulder, 1988
4 H. Bosch, 1982-1990
5 C. Smit, 1991
6 P. Weeda, 1992
7 Atelier PRO architekten, 1989
8 H. Klunder, 1990
9 Atelier PRO architekten, 1991
10 Soeters Van Eldonk Ponec architecten, 1997
11 de Architekten Cie./F. van Dongen, 2000

KNSM Island

83 Diener & Diener, 2001
84 Former captains' apartments KNSM, 1895
85 Villanova architecten, 1992
86 Hans Kollhoff en Christian Rapp, 1994
87 F. ten Holt, 1994
88 Studio-apartments in former KNSM canteen building
89 Bruno Albert, 1993
90 CASA Architecten, 1992
91 J. Coenen, 1997
92 J. Coenen, 1996
93 B. Galis, 1994
94 Quist Wintermans Architekten, 1994
95 Wiel Arets, 1996
96 Villanova architecten, 1991
97 Villanova architecten, 1997

Java Island

98 CASA Architecten, 1993
99 Jo Crepain Architect, 1995
100 Cruz & Ortiz, 1996
101 Rudy Uytenhaak architectenbureau, 1998
102 K. Christiaanse, 1997
103 Rudy Uytenhaak architectenbureau, 1998
104 Soeters Van Eldonk Ponec architecten, 1997
105 Cruz & Ortiz, 1996
106 Soeters Van Eldonk Ponec architecten, 1997
107 AWG Architecten / Groep 5, 1996
108 Geurst & Schulze architecten, 1996
109 AWG Architecten / Groep 5, 1996
110 Geurst & Schulze architecten, 1996
111 Meyer en Van Schooten Architecten, 2000
112 Geurst & Schulze architecten, 1996
113 AWG Architecten / Groep 5, 1996
114 K. Christiaanse, 1997
115 Rudy Uytenhaak architectenbureau, 1997
116 Cruz & Ortiz, 1996
117 K. Christiaanse, 1997
118 Rudy Uytenhaak architectenbureau, 1997
119 Soeters Van Eldonk Ponec architecten, 1999
120 Rudy Uytenhaak architectenbureau, 1997
121 K. Christiaanse, 1997
122 Soeters Van Eldonk Ponec architecten, 1997
123 K. Christiaanse, 1997
124 Cruz & Ortiz, 1996
125 Karelse Van der Meer Architecten, 1998

126 C. Nagelkerke, 1997
127 Karelse Van der Meer Architecten, 1998
128 Baneke Van der Hoeven Architekten, 1997
129 Karelse Van der Meer Architecten, 1998
130 Hotel
131 Karelse Van der Meer Architecten, 1999
132 Rudy Uytenhaak architectenbureau, 1997
133 S. Soeters, 1997
134 Cruz & Ortiz, 1996
135 KCAP, 1998
136 KCAP, 1998
137 S. Soeters, 1997
138 Cruz & Ortiz, 1996
139 S. Soeters, 1997
140 Rudy Uytenhaak architectenbureau, 1997
141 KCAP, 1998
142 Cruz & Ortiz, 1996
143 Cruz & Ortiz, 1996
144 Rudy Uytenhaak architectenbureau, 1997
145 Cruz & Ortiz, 1996
146 Geurst & Schulze architecten, 1996
147 Geurst & Schulze architecten, 1996
148 AWG Architecten / Groep 5, 1996
149 Geurst & Schulze architecten, 1996
150 KCAP, 1998
151 Karelse Van der Meer Architecten, 1999
152 C. Nagelkerke, 2000
153 Karelse Van der Meer Architecten, 1999
154 Baneke Van der Hoeven Architekten, 1998
155 Karelse Van der Meer Architecten, 1998
156 C. Nagelkerke, 1999
157 Karelse Van der Meer Architecten, 1999
158 Baneke Van der Hoeven Architekten, 1998
159 Karelse Van der Meer Architecten, 1999
160 Karelse Van der Meer Architecten, 1999
161 Atelier Zeinstra Van der Pol, 2001

a Brantasgracht

1 A. Zaaijer, 2000
2 C. Heuff, 2000
3 M. de Maeseneer, 2000
4 Architectenbureau Marlies Rohmer, 1999
5 J. van Eldonk, 1999
6 D. Ponec, 1999
7 R. van Zuuk, 2000
8 G.S. Kruunenberg, 2000
9 Bosch Architects, 1998
10 A. Zaaijer, 1999
11 Architectenbureau Marlies Rohmer, 1999
12 M. de Maeseneer, 1999
13 C. Heuff, 1999
14 R. van Zuuk, 1999
15 D. Ponec, 1999
16 J. van Eldonk, 1999

b Lamonggracht

1 M. de Maeseneer, 2000
2 R. van Zuuk, 2000
3 C. Heuff, 2000
4 J. van Eldonk, 1999
5 A. Zaaijer, 2000
6 Architectenbureau Marlies Rohmer, 1999
7 D. Ponec, 1999
8 Bosch Architects, 1998
9 G.S. Kruunenberg, 2000
10 Architectenbureau Marlies Rohmer, 1999
11 M. de Maeseneer, 2000
12 R. van Zuuk, 2000
13 C. Heuff, 2000
14 J. van Eldonk, 1999
15 D. Ponec, 2000
16 A. Zaaijer, 2000

c Majanggracht

1 B. Galis, 2000

2 D. van Gameren, 2000
3 B. Mastenbroek, 2000
4 B. Mastenbroek, 2000
5 Marx & Steketee, 2000
6 R. Onsia, 2000
7 W.H. Schenk, 2000
8 Marx & Steketee, 2000
9 B. Galis, 2000
10 Marx & Steketee, 2000
11 D. van Gameren, 2000
12 W.H. Schenk, 2000
13 Onix, 2000
14 Marx & Steketee, 2000
15 R. Onsia, 2000
16 D. de Meijer, 2000

d Seranggracht

1 D. de Meijer, 2000
2 D. van Gameren, 2000
3 R. Onsia, 2000
4 Marx & Steketee, 2000
5 W.H. Schenk, 2000
6 B. Mastenbroek, 2000
7 B. Mastenbroek, 2000
8 Marx & Steketee, 2000
9 D. de Meijer, 2000
10 W.H. Schenk, 2000
11 D. van Gameren, 2000
12 Marx & Steketee, 2000
13 Marx & Steketee, 2000
14 Onix, 2000
15 R. Onsia, 2000
16 B. Galis, 2000

Borneo and Sporenburg

12 Groos/De Jong Architecten / Atelier Z, Zavrel Architecten, 1994
13 Marge Architecten, 2000
14 Faro Architecten, 1998
15 Rudy Uytenhaak architectenbureau, 2001
16 Rudy Uytenhaak architectenbureau, 2001
17 Heren 5 Architecten, 2001
18 Architectenbureau K. van Velsen, 1999
19 CASA Architecten, 1999
20 Tupker/Van der Neut, 1997
21 S. Sorgdrager, 1999
22 Atelier Zeinstra van der Pol, 1998
23 Tupker/Van der Neut, 1999
24 Van Herk & De Kleijn architecten, 1999
25 MAP Architects, 1999

Scheepstimmermanstraat

26-2 Kwau with INBO Architecten, 2000
26-4 P. van der Klugt, 2001
26-6 R. de Prie, 1999
26-8 INBO Architecten, 2000
26-10/12 Kwau with INBO Architecten, 1999
26-14 INBO Architecten, 2000
26-16/18 Ruimtelab, 2000
26-20 Kwau with INBO Architecten, 1999
26-22 INBO Architecten, 2000
26-24 INBO Architecten, 2000
26-26 MVRDV, 2000
26-28 INBO Architecten, 2000
26-30 INBO Architecten, 2000
26-32 K. van Santen, 2000
26-34/36 Verheijen/Verkoren/De Haan, 2000
26-38 INBO Architecten, 2000
26-40 MVRDV, 1999
26-42 R. Petersma, 1999
26-44 INBO Architecten, 2000
26-46 H. Boogaard, 2000
26-48 C. Schrauwen, 1999
26-50 G. Prins, 2000
26-52 P. van der Klugt/G. Oorthuys, 2001
26-54 M. Tuerlings, 1999

Bottelierplein

26-2/4 Tekton Architecten, 2003

Scheepstimmermanstraat

27-56/58 N. van Slobbe, 1999
27-60 BEB Architecten, 1998
27-62 Höhne & Rapp, 2000
27-64 E. Rahantoknam, 1999
27-66 Orbit, 1999
27-68 Höhne & Rapp, 2000
27-70 de Architectengroep/D. van Gameren, 2000
27-72/74 G. Oorthuys/M. Elbers, 2000
27-76 J. Puister, 1999
27-78 Faro Architecten, 1997
27-80/82 Heren 5 Architecten, 2000
27-84 J. Fraijman, 1999
27-86 W. van Seumeren, 1999
27-88/92 H. Tupker, 1999
27-94 R. Petersma, 1999
27-96 CASA Architecten, 2000
27-98 Buro de Binnenstad/J. Fraijman, 2000
27-100 INBO Architecten, 2000
27-102 S. Rektorik, 1999
27-104 L. Lousberg, 1999
27-106 J. Puister, 1999
27-108 de Architectengroep/B. Mastenbroek, 2000
27-110 Heren 5 Architecten, 2000
27-112 H.J.B. Slawik, 2001
27-114 Kwau, 2000
27-116 Faro Architecten, 1999
27-118 Kwau, 1999
27-120 Architectenbureau K. van Velsen, 1999
27-122 H. J. Duyzer, 1999
27-124 M. de Reus, 1999
27-126 Architectuurstudio Hertzberger, 1999
27-128 G. Daan, 1999
27-130 Kingma Roorda architecten, 1998
27-132 Rau & Partners, 2000
28 de Architectengroep/B. Mastenbroek/ D. van Gameren, 1999
29 E. Miralles, 1999
30 E. Miralles, 1999
31 K. Christiaanse, 1998
32 Tupker/Van der Neut, 1997
33 Atelier Zeinstra Van der Pol, 1999
34 S. Sorgdrager, 1999
35 Tupker/Van der Neut, 1997
36 Architectenbureau Marlies Rohmer, 2000
37 CASA Architecten, 1997
38 Van Sambeek en Van Veen, 2000
39 Claus en Kaan Architecten, 2000
40 Köther & Salman Architekten, 1999
41 Van Sambeek en Van Veen, 2000
42 de Architekten Cie./F. van Dongen, 2001
43 Stuurman Partners, school, 1997
44 Atelier Zeinstra van der Pol, 1999
45 JHK (De Jong Hoogveld De Kat), 2000
46 Claus en Kaan Architecten, 2000
47 Claus en Kaan Architecten, 2000
48 JHK (De Jong Hoogveld De Kat), 2000
49 DKV architekten, 1997
50 UN Studio, 1999
51 Ruimtelab, 1999
52 Rempt van der Donk Architekten, 2000
53 Höhne & Rapp, 2001
54 Atelier Zeinstra van der Pol, 1999
55 DKV architekten, 1997
56 Claus en Kaan Architecten, 2000
57 Claus en Kaan Architecten, 2000
58 M3H architecten, 1998
59 Heren 5 Architecten, 1999
60 Van Sambeek en Van Veen, 1998
61 Höhne & Rapp, 2001
62 Van Sambeek en Van Veen, 1998
63 DKV architekten, 1997
64 Neutelings Riedijk Architecten, 1997
65 Neutelings Riedijk Architecten, 1999
66 R. Visser, 1997
67 Köther & Salman Architekten, 1996

B

C

D

Java-eiland

129 128 127 126 125
124 123 122 121
120
Sumatrakade

131 136 a 119 118 117 116 115 114 113 112 111
132 133 142 143 150 145
16 134 135 137 138 139 140 141 144 146 147 148 149 151 152 153 154 155

Javakade

162
163 164
Oostelijke Handelskade
166
167
168
4

a (L) 9 t/m 16 ↓
a (R) 1 t/m 8 ↑
3

b (L) 9 t/m 16 ↓
b (R) 1 t/m 8 ↑
3

c (L) 9 t/m 16 ↓
c (R) 1 t/m 8 ↑
3

Piet Heinkade
165 171 169 173 170
172
174

IJ-haven

2

175 176
178
177
179

180

3

Piet Heinkade

Rietlanden

4

5

Het IJ

KNSM-eiland

Sporenburg

Borneo-eiland

Piet Heintunnel

Entrepothaven

Borneo-eiland

Veemarktterrein

Abattoirterrein

Surinamekade

KNSM-laan

Azartplein

Bogortuin

Levantkade

J.F. van Hengelstraat

Ertskade

Stuurmankade

Scheepstimmermanstraat

Stokerkade

Panamakade

Borneokade

C. de Boerlaan

Rietlandterras

Borneolaan

Entrepot-West

Borneokade

Entrepothof

Van Eesterenlaan

Veelaan

Zeeburgerkade

Cruquiusweg

H.A.J.M. Baanderskade

   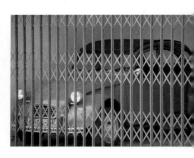

The inhabitants
Sabine Lebesque

Bianca 35, gynaecologist in training
Merlijn 35, pediatrician in training
Ruben 2
baby on the way

location **KNSM-laan, KNSM Island**
surface area **120 m², including built-in**
conservatory
price **233,700 euro, parking space**
22,700 euro

What kind of dwelling do you have?
'The flat was sold to us on paper as a
"duo dwelling", which is supposed to
mean that two single people would be
living here together. That's why there
are two large living/sleeping areas, with
a conservatory and kitchen intended
for communal use in between. There is
also another smaller room and a laundry
room, bathroom and separate toilet.
As a family, we immediately adapted
the layout by making an extra children's
room in the hall, which was initially quite
large. For that matter it's all families in
this block. None of them use their flat
the way it was designed.'

Where did you come from?
'We lived together in a 70 m² flat in
De Pijp; Merlijn's father had initially
bought it as a student flat 15 years
earlier, and we later bought it from him.
We were able to sell that flat for 199,700
euro, at the height of the market two
years ago. With all the costs of moving,
parquet floors, kitchen and the like, we
have now spent 299,500 euro on the
new flat.'

*Why did you choose the Eastern
Harbour District?*
'That was a coincidence. We were looking
at various places in the city at the time,
but we were never high enough on the
list. A friend offered us her spot on the
waiting list for this complex. She also

knew the contractor. Perhaps it was
luck, but we came out third in the lottery.
At the time we didn't think the Eastern
Harbour District was very nice; everything was barren and unfinished. Only
later, as it became more of a neighbourhood, did we start to like it.
As far as the architecture goes, we think
our block is the least beautiful in the
area, or to put it another way, the least
special; it's quite no-nonsense and plain.
The Whale, opposite from us, we think
is the ugliest. Piraeus, but also the
Javakade as a whole, we think are most
successful. That really was made into
something special.'

How do you see your housing career?
'We think we'll move to a different home
in about five years, preferably with a
garden. We're keeping an eye on what's
going on with the Zeeburgereiland, for
instance. But everything depends on our
work. We're both training to qualify as
medical specialists, and if an offer for
a job outside the city comes along, that
will determine our choice.'

Esther 34, sociologist
Peter 39, historian
Pauline 1

location **Javakade, Java Island**
surface area **104 m², including balcony**
price **820 euro rent, garage 50 euro**

What kind of dwelling do you have?
'As far as we know this flat doesn't have
a name. We live on the top floor of this
apartment building, which combines
maisonettes and smaller and larger
apartments. Our flat has three small
rooms, a large living room with kitchen, a
large bathroom, separate toilet, laundry
room and a very sunny balcony. We had
a closet built in the hallway, which cuts
off the direct access to the kitchen,
which we reach via the living room.'

Where did you come from?
Peter moved in with Esther a few years
ago in the flat she owned in the Nieuwmarkt quarter, made up of two small
storeys each 20 m² in size. 'We quickly
went in search of something bigger,
although there were no concrete plans
to have children at the time. That was
not an issue then. We were looking in
the private-sector rental market, since
we were not eligible for public-sector
housing and buying was not an option,
because neither of us had a permanent
job.'

*Why did you choose the Eastern
Harbour District?*
Esther: 'Initially I didn't want to leave the
Nieuwmarkt quarter at all, not so much
because I thought everything about the
area was fantastic, but because I think
it's difficult to move and have to adapt
to a new environment. When we saw this
rental flat for the first time – bare and
dirty from the previous tenants – we
didn't jump at it either. We also thought

the composition of the resident
population here was too one-dimensional – ladies who played tennis, white
men with glasses of white wine. Later w
thoroughly studied the floor plan at our
leisure, and we were forced to conclud
that we couldn't pass up an apartment
on the top floor, with a lift, a big south-
facing balcony and a lot of square
metres. We decided to significantly
renovate the whole thing; with coloured
walls and a light floor covering, we wer
able to make the flat what we wanted.
The floor plan is also very economically
and conveniently laid out.'

How do you see your housing career?
'We talk about that sometimes, but not
in very concrete terms. We signed up fo
IJburg when the time came, but we feel
absolutely no inclination to move out
there. Of course a garden would be nic
and our financial situation is more stabl
than when we moved into this flat, so
buying is a possibility. But for the rent
we pay, you don't get very much in the
ower-occupied sector, compared to
what we have now.
We're starting to feel an attachment to
the neighbourhood. Air, space, and quit
respectable, decent people are positive
points. Peter's parents, now living in
the east of the country, are even on the
lookout for an apartment here on the
Java Island at the moment.'

nne 44, graphic designer
4

n Scheepstimmermanstraat, Borneo
e area **113 m²**, including balcony
47,500 euro

kind of dwelling do you have?
a friend who is an architect, I
ned a house myself on a private
l and built two apartments in it, each
o levels. My flat in the lower section
oms that can be closed off on two
on the street side; the rear section,
he kitchen and living quarters, is
lly connected by a roomy empty
e that creates a ceiling height of five
es.'

re did you come from?
ormer official residence was a flat in
jp, in public-sector rental housing.
't think it was any place to have a
, not so much because of the neigh-
hood but because of a weird neigh-
But as a small-scale freelancer
an irregular income I didn't see any
ce of moving, initially. My accountant
ed me to compare the costs of a
o and flat with buying a house in
h I could work as well as live, in the
-subsidized owner-occupied sector
was attractive at the time. When I
looking in earnest the subsidized
turned out to have gone up, and
e was an opportunity to register for
rcel here on Borneo. Then I thought,
an build two apartments there on one
el, maybe it's doable. Although I
starting from the cheapest options
had to keep increasing my budget
ughout the design and building
ess, it all worked out.
ught in the buyers of the other apart-
almost immediately. During the
truction, I lived in my studio with
, who was a baby at the time, as a

transition phase for two years, while my
partner had his own house outside the
city, and still does.'

*Why did you choose the Eastern
Harbour District?*
'When I saw the urban plan for Borneo
and Sporenburg, with all these little
houses and such a powerful element
as the water all around, it immediately
appealed to me, and I also thought, "not
much can go wrong here". Furthermore
the area provides an opportunity to
combine housing and work in the same
place, which is what I was looking for.
And that's not just true of the private
parcels but also of the other houses on
this island.'

*What does your housing career
look like?*
'Although building my own house was a
very intense process, in which was so
personally involved, I want to do it again,
preferably with the same friend/architect.
That's why I've signed up for a parcel on
IJburg. I haven't yet worked out whether
it's actually financially feasible; we'll see.
Otherwise I'm very content here, the way
a child can grow up, the school nearby,
playing in the street and a lot of contact
with the other residents of the neighbourhood. Every once in a while it dawns on
me that I'm living on a 100 percent white,
luxury island cut off from the rest of
society, not really a cross-section of the
real world. And what drives me nuts are
the people in little boats who want to
take a peek inside my house every five
minutes, the whole summer long. I hope
the novelty will have worn off this coming
summer and that they'll keep sailing on
to IJburg.'

Eireen 34, architect
Wouter 35, architect
Lena 1

location **Venetiëhof, KNSM Island**
surface area **85 m²**, excluding balcony
price **800 euro rent**, including garage parking
space, sublet for 200 euro

What kind of dwelling do you have?
'We have a gallery flat with three rooms
on the fourth floor, with a balcony on
the northwest side. The flat is spacious
but rather noisy, and the balcony is
pretty windy, so you can't sit there very
comfortably.'

Where did you come from?
'We were living temporarily in a sublet in
Oud-West, in a 40 m² flat. When we had
to leave, with me in an advanced stage of
pregnancy as well, I searched fanatically
for a flat in Amsterdam, because we
both work here. I really rang up everyone
all over the place until I finally got a bite
with the investor/project developer for
this complex, who rents out a number of
flats himself. I signed the contract before
I'd even seen the flat.'

Why the Eastern Harbour District?
'This was the only place where we could
get anything. We think the neighbourhood's ok, as it happens. One good
quality is that it is quiet and not run-down.
The location on the water is unique.
The downside is that it's rather dull and
that there are no places to meet here on
the island. The Brazilië shopping centre is
very limited, so I usually do the shopping
on Saturday in and around the Javastraat
in the Dapper quarter. Sometimes I think
this place is just like a Vinex neighbourhood in Amsterdam.
In our building, there are mostly older
people and couples without children.

What you notice is that they don't make
the building their own, the way you see
it in other places in the Eastern Harbour
District. There are few planters on the
galleries and people rarely sit on the
benches in the inner courtyard. I actually
know only one fellow resident by name,
the neighbour to whom we sublet our
parking space.'

*What does your housing career
look like?*
At the end of this year we're moving back
to the Ouden Westen area in Rotterdam,
to the complex we once squatted. We
developed it in association with the city
along with the other residents as a private
commission. Our own home will be 210 m²
distributed over three floors. We're very
busy with the construction at the moment.
In fact we're expats like many of the
people in Emerald Empire – transient and
anonymous.'

Nynke 36, architect
Jan 37, industrial designer
Daan 3
Guusje 2

location **Ertskade, Sporenburg**
surface area **105 m², after renovation 120 m²,**
extra garage a short distance away
price **140,700 euro, garage 9,075 euro**

What kind of dwelling do you have?
'We have an open patio dwelling on
two and half levels, and a private carport
shut off from the street by a metal gate.
When we bought this home seven years
ago off the blueprints, the plan was to
enclose the carport, so we bought an
extra garage at the same time. The city
did not give us planning permission for
this, but after long negotiations we did
add a room in a section of the carport, in
cooperation with the architect. A lot of
other residents followed our example.'

Where did you come from?
'We rented in the private sector on the
Nicolaas Witsekade. We were looking to
buy a home for which we didn't want to
spend more than what we were paying
on rent. I specifically did not want to
ever end up having to work to pay off
a mortgage. Housing in the older part of
the city didn't appeal to us or was above
the budget we'd set ourselves.'

*Why did you choose the Eastern
Harbour District?*
'During the urban-planning preparations,
it immediately struck me as a fabulous
plan. We immediately chose the
Ertskade, initially for the conservatory
dwellings by Willem Jan Neutelings, but
these must have been sold privately,
because we never saw them offered up
for public sale. We'd lost out in the
lottery for these homes by Köther and
Salman until someone unexpectedly

dropped out when construction had
already begun. So we didn't have to wait
so long before it was finished. We were
lucky in that it was our favourite type,
with the three levels on the north side
and two on the south side, so that
there's a lot of sunlight on the patio.
The success of this neighbourhood, as
far as I'm concerned, is the fact that the
streets are dead-ends; there's nowhere
you can get to, so you only come here
if you have good reason to. That creates
a village-like social control, which is
quite comforting for families with small
children. Most people come from the city
centre, many from the Jordaan, so that
they're used to a certain street life. In the
summer I definitely get a sense of being
on a summer holiday when I get home.
Residents dive right off the dock into the
water, and people barbecue until late in
the evening.'

*What does your housing career
look like?*
'We really enjoy it here, but still we are
looking for something else. We've had
an estate agent on the job for three
years. The house is not big enough for
the children, and there's not a lot of
room left for extensions. Jan also works
outside the city. When you factor in
IJburg, the traffic jams on the ring are
only going to get worse. So we're
looking in Zuid, that will save at least
half an hour twice a day.
So we're keeping all options open for
when something nice comes our way.'

Marianne 42, civil servant with the DMB

location **C.J.K. van Aalststraat, Sporenburg**
surface area **82 m², 12 m² roof terrace**
price **400 euro rent**

What kind of dwelling do you have?
'This a three-room rental flat distributed
over four levels in the public sector.
I have my own entrance on the street,
with a storage space, a bedroom with a
shower stall on the first floor, the kitchen
and a bedroom with a toilet on the
second floor and the sitting room with
terrace on the third floor. I got the flat
because of the duration of occupancy
I'd built up on the housing association's
waiting list.'

Where did you come from?
I lived in a renovated two-room flat in
the Transvaal quarter. I was looking for
another flat because I had the feeling
I had entered a new phase in my life.
I was and for that matter still am very
attached to my old neighbourhood, close
to the Amstel Station and the Linaeus-
straat. Now that I live here, I've realized
that older buildings entail a lot of noise
nuisance, which I accepted at the time,
but which I'm glad to be free of.'

Why the Eastern Harbour District?
'That was not a conscious choice.
I looked for about three years and at
a certain point began to realize that,
because of a change to the waiting-list
system, my number ended up lower.
That was a signal to get going.
When I became eligible for this flat I
really investigated objectively whether
the neighbourhood appealed to me. At
night, after I'd been out, I went looking
around the street. The peace and quiet
especially appealed to me.
The majority of the buildings and layout
really appeals to me. The fact that the

population is so white creates a
recognizable lifestyle. This means I do
have so much of a sense that my under
standing is always being called upon,
although to my own eyes that seems
completely politically incorrect.
Unlike some of the neighbourhood
residents, I am very happy about the
children's playground here in the stree
I think that you sometimes have to
respect the effort the city is making to
offer something to the great number of
children here. It brings the neighbourhood to life.'

*What does your housing career
look like?*
'I think I'll stay here until I'm 60, althou
I do have to be realistic about the stair
in the house. The shower and toilet are
not on the same floor, nor are the kitch
and sitting room, so the house forces
you to move. That's very healthy, of
course, but just now that I happen to
have a leg injury, I'm noticing what a
chore it can be.'